JOURNEY THROUGH
INDONESIA

TIM HANNIGAN

TUTTLE Publishing

Tokyo | Rutland, Vermont | Singapore

CONTENTS

FRONT ENDPAPERS First light at Pura Ulun Danu Tamblingan, a Hindu temple on the shores of a crater lake in the volcanic highlands of Bali.

PAGE 1 A man from the tiny island of Rote near Timor shows off the island's traditional *ikat* fabric, lontar palm headgear and iconic musical instrument, the *sasandu*.

PAGES 2–3 The mighty Gunung Merapi volcano dwarfs the Borobudur temple and dominates the landscapes of Central Java at dawn.

dakan

Indonesia

N

500 km
200 miles

Talaud Is.

Sangihe Is.

Manado ✈ ★ Tangkoko
Batuangus
Nature Reserve

Morotai I.

Halmahera I.

Gorontalo ■ Sofifi

★ Togian Islands

Bacan I. Raja Ampat ★ *Waigeo I.*

Manokwari ■

Biak I.

Palu ■

S U L A W E S I

Salawati I.

Obi I.

Yapen I.

nuju

Banggai Islands

Sula Islands

M a l u k u I s.

Misool I.

Jayapura ■

Toraja ★

Buru I.

Seram I.

P A P U A

Baliem ★
Valley

Pare Pare

Kendari ■

Ambon ■

Timika ●

Kassar ✈

Buton I.

Banda Is.

Asmat Region ★

Selayar I.

Aru Is.

ambora
n

Damar Is.

Yamdena I.

Yos Sudarso I.

nbawa I. *Flores I.*

Adonara I.

Wetar I.

Merauke ●

Komodo I. ★ *Rinca I.*

Pantar I. *Alor I.* DILI

Komodo
Nat. Park

T I M O R

Sumba I.

Kupang ■

A GALAXY OF ISLANDS

Strung across the equator in an arabesque of emerald islands, Indonesia is a nation like no other. From the northernmost tip of Sumatra to the jungle borders of Papua New Guinea, it spans a distance of more than 3,000 miles (4,830 km). The space between these distant points is filled with myriad languages, landscapes and cultures. It is a single country with all the diversity of an entire continent.

From ancestor-worshipping communities in misty green mountains to the sea-level stilt villages of maritime wanderers, and from the urban mayhem of Medan to the sophisticated holiday playgrounds of Bali, every facet of Indonesia has its counterpoint, its contrast. With 17,508 individual islands by the latest official count, this is the world's greatest archipelago, a place offering a lifetime of journeys. Whether your own point of departure is London or New York, Singapore or Sydney, or indeed Jakarta or Surabaya, there is a limitless supply of new landfalls out there amongst the islands.

The Indonesian archipelago was born of fantastic geological violence some 70 million years ago. The main southern island arc, stretching from Sumatra southeastwards through Java, Bali and Nusa Tenggara, traces the line of the impact zone where the Indo-Australian tectonic plate drives beneath the Sunda Plate. This ongoing collision is what created these landmasses and what powers the palpable sense of turbulence still underpinning Indonesia's geography. This is a place where mountain skylines trail thin streamers of smoke from their highest summits, where the surface is fractured and the earth seems to breathe in sulfur-scented gouts, and where the soil itself seems to have a tremulous, palpitating heartbeat.

LEFT While much of Indonesia is dominated by volcanic land-scapes, the Fam Islands, part of the Raja Ampat archipelago off the northwestern coast of Papua, are made up of limestone karst. This ancient sedimentary rock, carved into fantastical shapes by the action of water over millions of years, consists of the petrified remains of prehistoric coral reefs. There's a remarkable geological continuity in Raja Ampat, for beneath the surface, in the shadow of the ancient fossils, lie some of the finest living reefs in Indonesia.

Volcano Nation

Indonesia has more volcanoes than any other country on earth. There are well over a hundred volcanic peaks considered active by geologists and hundreds more that are currently dormant. A jagged spine of smoking summits stretches along the entire length of Sumatra, Java, Bali and Nusa Tenggara, fueled by material forced down into the earth's mantle at the plate subduction zone, which lies beneath the Indian Ocean offshore. Other individual volcanoes are scattered throughout the more disorderly array of islands to the north.

Many of these volcanoes are in a permanent state of low-level activity, sulfurous smoke continuously issuing from their craters, and most years at least one of their number kicks off with a bout of heightened action. Flight schedules disrupted by volcanic ash clouds are a fact of life in Indonesia. Once in a while there is a more serious eruption. That of Gunung Merapi in Java in 2010 was one of the most dramatic in recent years. Fortunately, however, nothing in current lifetimes has matched the devastation wrought during the two catastrophic explosions of the nineteenth century: Tambora and Krakatau.

The destructive power, distinctive forms and fertility-fueling mineral run-offs of the volcanoes have given them an important place in many traditional cultures in Indonesia. They are homes of gods and ancestral spirits, architectural reference points and a permanent imaginative presence, glowering on the horizon.

ABOVE Krakatau, often misspelt Krakatoa, is a byword for volcanic devastation, thanks to its catastrophic 1883 eruption, which killed around 35,000 people and affected weather patterns around the world in the months that followed. The island volcano, in the strait between Java and Sumatra, is still sporadically active today.

To the north of the Indian Ocean-facing islands lies a less orderly rank of landmasses. The vast, forested thumbprint of Borneo, divided between Malaysia and Brunei in the north and the Indonesian provinces of Kalimantan in the south, the wild knot of Sulawesi and the scattered outposts of Maluku, all run eastwards before the entire archipelago draws together at Indonesia's easternmost anchor, the huge hulk of Papua, a frontier in every sense of the word.

This galaxy of islands is, for the most part, a place of furious fecundity. During the northern winter, bruise-colored, water-laden weather systems from the South China Sea sweep down across the archipelago and the monsoon downpours they unload provide more than enough moisture to see the place through the other half of the year when the trade winds shift and dry air from the red heart of Australia brushes across the country. The deep, damp volcanic soils, meanwhile, give out an endless round of growth cycles, be it in the sculpted rice terraces of Java and Lombok or in the primeval forest of the Sumatran hinterland. Green is the color scheme here, set against a shifting ocean of the deepest blue.

BELOW The Mahakam River cuts a snakelike swathe through the lowlands of East Kalimantan, Borneo. The rivers of Borneo are ancient cultural conduits, linking the inland Dayak communities with the trading sultanates of the coast.

RIGHT Volcanic geography makes for life at extreme angles. Farming communities, such as this one near Dieng in Central Java, exploit the superbly fertile soils and plentiful rainfall through formidable feats of terracing.

A NATION OF VILLAGES AND CLANS

A quarter of a billion people call Indonesia home and in this, the fourth most populous country on earth, their lifestyles span the entire gamut of human existence. In the sophisticated megalopolises of Java there are young professionals living at the cutting edge of the digital twenty-first century, while in the deepest reaches of the Papuan forest there are tribes still shunning all contact with the outside world.

ABOVE From the temple artisans of the classical past to these contemporary pavement artists offering a fine line in landscape and portraiture in Bogor, a hill town south of Jakarta, Indonesia's artistic traditions run deep.
LEFT Indonesia's big cities are home to young, confident and increasingly affluent societies. Modern urbanites embrace all the leisure and social activities of their counterparts across the world, as in Jakarta's annual 3-mile (5-km) Color Run.
BELOW Twenty-first-century life does not necessarily mean an end to a strong sense of cultural identity among Indonesia's myriad minorities. Many of the Dayak people of Kalimantan still proudly maintain elements of their traditional heritage in the modern world.

Very broadly speaking, most Indonesians fall into two distinct ethnic groups. In the easternmost regions the indigenous people are Melanesians, dark-skinned, curly haired and descended from the first migrants to move into the archipelago around 40,000 years ago. Further west, meanwhile, most people are descended from much later settlers: the Austronesians, who arrived within the last 5,000 years, bringing with them the seeds of many of Indonesia's traditional cultures.

But that's just the start of the story. There are well over 200 languages in Indonesia and numberless dialects, though these days almost everyone also speaks Bahasa Indonesia, the official national language. However, in all this glorious diversity there are certain common threads. Outside of the deepest jungles of Papua and Kalimantan, where a few people still lead deeply traditional hunter-gather lifestyles, Indonesia is fundamentally a nation of villages and settled agriculture. Be it a neat cluster of stone-built homes with red-tiled roofs in the prosperous rice-growing heartlands of Java or Bali, or a high huddle of traditional clan houses built of bamboo and thatch in the dry, hard-scrabble outlands of Sumba or Timor, the compact rural community is the lodestar of Indonesian culture. This is where traditional crafts and belief systems are kept strongest. When Indonesians, even those living high-rise lives in the capital, talk about making a return visit to their ancestral home they speak of *pulang kampung*, "going home to the village". Even in the cities, the institutions and atmosphere of the village endures in the working-class neighborhoods, also known as *kampung*, just like their countryside equivalents, with their powerful sense of community.

Migrant Minorities

Indonesia has been attracting settlers from distant shores for many centuries. Some married into the existing populations and vanished into the great melting pot of the archipelago. But others created enduring communities of their own. In many of the grand old port cities there are small groups of Indonesian Arabs, descendants of Yemeni traders in spice and sandalwood who arrived in centuries past. In a few places in Sumatra there are also communities of Indian Tamils, and a handful of families in Maluku and Nusa Tenggara can still trace Portuguese ancestry.

But by far the most significant immigrant-descended minority is the Chinese. Indonesia has been connected to China through trade since prehistory and Chinese settlers have been making new homes in Southeast Asia for hundreds and probably thousands of years, adding dashes of influence to local languages, cuisines and architectural styles. During the colonial era, immigration increased as Chinese entrepreneurs and laborers helped to build the framework of a modern archipelago-wide economy. Today Chinese Indonesians live and work throughout the country and Chinese temples still make for incense-wreathed dashes of blood-red color in the old port districts of many towns and cities.

ABOVE Indonesia's Chinese minority has often been subject to discrimination down the decades and many Chinese cultural activities were once officially outlawed. Today, however, *Imlek*, the local name for Chinese New Year, is a public holiday, celebrated with panache as here in Solo, Central Java.

ABOVE Village boys wear clothes that double as a badge of faith. Conventional Muslim dress for men in Indonesia consists of sarong, collarless shirt and skullcap. Amongst adults a white skullcap signifies that the wearer has completed the Haj pilgrimage to Mecca, though for children it's usually simply part of the semi-formal uniform of a koranic school. **OPPOSITE TOP** Courtiers from the Kraton of Yogyakarta in Java wait patiently during a court ceremony. The Javanese account for the single biggest group in Indonesia, approximately 100 million people.

As well as a mosaic of languages, ethnicities and cultures, Indonesia is also a complex patchwork of religions. It's best known as "the world's most populous Muslim-majority nation", and the fact that densely populated Java, home to over half the entire Indonesian population, along with most of the major urban centers elsewhere, have Muslim majorities means that around 87 percent of Indonesians identify as Muslim. But on the map the split is much more equitable and large swathes of the more sparsely populated east have Catholic or Protestant majorities. Bali, famously, is a bastion of a unique local version of Hinduism, and there are pockets of Buddhism here and there around the country. What's more, official religious designations often sit side by side with older indigenous belief systems. In many parts of Nusa Tenggara, ancient traditions of ancestor veneration have been incorporated alongside more recent adherence to Islam, Protestantism or Catholicism under the designation of *adat* or "custom". In Tana Toraja in Sulawesi, locals combine enthusiastic church-going with strict adherence to funeral rites rooted in the pre-Christian *Aluk Todolo* beliefs, while Java is home to the syncretic *Kejawen* tradition.

Their homeland is the eastern two-thirds of the island of Java, but they are also found in transmigrant communities around the archipelago. Yogyakarta, with its ruling sultan and refined traditions of art and language, is often regarded as the Javanese cultural capital. **RIGHT** On the slopes of the Gunung Gede volcano, just 30 miles (48 km) from the skyscrapers of central Jakarta, rural life continues much as it has for centuries. In the rice-farming village of Rumpin, a local woman dressed in traditional batik stokes a cooking fire in a kitchen walled with woven bamboo.

ABOVE Local men put on a dramatic performance in a village in the southern coastal lowlands of Papua. This remote region is the homeland of the Asmat people. The Asmat once had a fierce reputation for warfare, but today they are best known for their elaborate wood carvings, many linked to ancestor venerating traditions.

RIGHT By no means all Indonesian Muslims are strict in their adherence to the five times a day prayer routine of Islam, but the communal prayers that mark the end of the Ramadan fasting month draw huge crowds to mosques everywhere. Those at Jakarta's central Istiqlal Mosque, seen here, are amongst the biggest.

TOP An old lady in Bogor, West Java, takes it easy. Not everyone in Java is ethnically Javanese. Most people in Bogor and across the western part of the island are Sundanese.

ABOVE *Reog Ponorogo* is a masked dance with associations of supernatural power, hailing from the East Java town of Ponorogo. The cultural identity of the town is intimately tied up with the dance.

LEFT In the historic quarter of Yogyakarta in Java, two young local women strike a casual pose. Commonly known as Yogya (pronounced "Jogja"), this royal city is widely regarded as the cultural capital of Java, home to its most refined linguistic and artistic traditions and bastion of a pronounced cultural identity.

ABOVE Java is synonymous with coffee and cups of the stuff, served unfiltered, sweet and black, have long fueled conversations in bamboo-built roadside cafés across the island. These days, however, urban Java, along with the rest of the country, has latched on to New York-style café culture in a big way, as these Jakarta baristas know well.

The Sea People

Indonesia is a nation of islands where most people turn their backs to the sea, with cultures rooted in rice fields and forests. But there are some Indonesians who have made the ocean their own.

An elegant white schooner with a high prow making stately progress across a cobalt-blue sea is a classic image of Indonesia. These boats, generically known as *pinisi*, are the traditional craft of the Bugis, mighty seafarers from southern Sulawesi who have traditionally dominated Indonesia's interisland trade routes. Though most Bugis still live in the region around Makassar, their voyages have carried them far and wide and there are distinct Bugis communities in coastal regions all over Indonesia and even beyond, in Malaysia and Singapore. In precolonial centuries Bugis sailors made it as far as the northern coasts of Australia to barter with local Aboriginals.

The other fabled seafarers of the archipelago are the Bajau, a shadowy, tide-borne tribe sometimes described as "sea gypsies". Living in scattered coastal communities everywhere from the southern Philippines to Timor, the Bajau traditionally spent their entire lives on the water. Today most live ashore, though a few still cleave to the old ways out amongst the small islands south of Sulawesi.

ABOVE In a few places, especially around the coasts of Sulawesi and Borneo, communities of Bajau still live as they have always done in villages built on stilts straight out of the water, with local children taking to boats at an early age.

CURRENTS OF THE PAST

The past is out in the open in Indonesia. On high Javanese mountainsides market gardeners tend their tidy plots in the shadow of sculpture-encrusted thousand-year-old temples, and in down-at-heel harbor towns all over the archipelago a rank of mildewed Doric columns here and a heavyset hipped roof there still speak of untold spice fortunes earned in the age of sail.

BELOW The Hindu-Buddhist past has left Java richly studded with tangible traces of the past, and nowhere more so than at the mighty Prambanan complex in Central Java, built in the ninth century by the Hindu Sanjaya dynasty. Another hidden history is also revealed here. By the nineteenth century the temples were in ruins, the central structures were swamped with vegetation and many smaller shrines had collapsed entirely. Dutch colonialists organized early clean-up operations, but it was only in the 1930s that restoration work got properly underway, work still continuing today as the piles of masonry awaiting reconstruction demonstrate.

RIGHT Although the international sea lanes have long since been taken over by modern freighters, much of the maritime traffic between the smaller ports of Indonesia is still undertaken by wooden boats. Most of these boats, which carry cargoes of everything from cement to instant noodles, are now motorized but they are still built to the template of the *pinisi*, a two-masted sailing vessel traditionally built by the Bugis shipwrights of southern Sulawesi, long the center of seafaring culture in the archipelago. Large numbers of these boats can be seen loading up with cargo at Jakarta's Sunda Kelapa wharf.

The abiding theme of Indonesia's past has been maritime contact. The country lies at one of the world's greatest trading junctions, a halfway house between India and the Middle East to the west and China and Japan to the east, and with its own rich array of island produce waiting for shipment to the four corners. Over the millennia dhows, junks, carracks and schooners from all directions have dropped anchor off Indonesia's coasts, unloading new ideas and new religions along with their cargoes of trade goods.

In the early centuries of the current era the seeds of Hinduism and Buddhism from India germinated in the entrepôt states of Java, Sumatra and Kalimantan and a uniquely Indonesian Hindu-Buddhist culture developed, with local god-kings presiding over trading empires and commanding epic temple-building projects. The apogee of this Indian-inspired epoch came in the mighty Majapahit Empire, which ruled from Java between the fourteenth and sixteenth centuries. Its influence still lingers in the archipelago today.

Eventually new merchants and adventurers, following trade winds from the far side of the Indian Ocean, began to appear in the ports of Indonesia, bringing a new creed with them, and as

The Language of History

Though Indonesia has hundreds of distinct local languages and dialects, just about everyone from one end of the country to the other also speaks Bahasa Indonesia. Also known simply as "Indonesian", this official national language is a modernized version of Malay, for centuries the lingua franca of maritime Southeast Asia and also still spoken in slightly different form as Bahasa Melayu in neighboring Malaysia.

Though it is part of the Austronesian language family, Bahasa Indonesia has sucked up loanwords like a sponge over the centuries and today it is like a living dictionary of the myriad foreign influences that have affected Indonesia. The Indonesian word for bread, *roti*, is of Indian origin, but the word for butter, *mentega*, comes from Portuguese—a telltale indication of who most likely introduced those particular foodstuffs to the region. Its vocabulary is also heavily laden with borrowings from Sanskrit and Arabic. It is peppered with bits and pieces from Chinese languages and it also has a few specks of Persian and more besides, not to mention all sorts of technical terminology imported from Dutch and English.

ABOVE The figurehead of Indonesia's struggle for nationhood against the Dutch colonial authorities was Sukarno, depicted here on an early stamp. Born in Surabaya in 1901, he rose through the ranks of the nationalist movement and eventually became the country's first president. His charisma and crowd-pleasing oration style were legendary. **TOP RIGHT** The city now called Jakarta was known to the Dutch as Batavia. Although it has long since grown into a sprawling megalopolis, the heart of the old colonial settlement, founded in 1619, survives in the area known as Kota. Old Dutch warehouses still flank the river here.

Majapahit declined Islam became the dominant religion in the western regions of the archipelago, albeit an Islam often laced with traces of the Hindu-Buddhism and indigenous ancestor-worship that went before.

Hot on the heels of the Muslim traders came Europeans, seeking out the same astronomically expensive spices that grew only in the fragrant groves of Maluku—Portuguese in the early sixteenth century and then Dutch and English sailors a hundred years later. It was the Dutch who eventually came to dominate the spice market, and over the coming centuries they turned their trading company into an empire, holding sway over the region that they knew as the East Indies. All empires come to an end eventually, of course, and after the brutal experience of Japanese occupation during World War II, followed by the firestorm of an anti-colonial revolution, Indonesia became the independent nation that it remains today.

No new chapter in Indonesian history has ever managed to erase the traces of what went before, and the past here is not only to be found in ruins and relics. It is also a living, breathing thing. History runs through the patterns of the batik and *ikat* cloth. It underscores the rhythms of the archipelago's musical traditions. It adds spice to the language and flavor to the food, and its tangled traces inform the architecture of Balinese temples and Javanese mosques alike.

ABOVE The foundations of European colonialism in Indonesia were laid by the *Vereenigde Oostindische Compagnie*, the Dutch East India Company, better known as the VOC. Founded in 1602 to monopolize the lucrative trade in spices from Maluku, the company had what may have been the world's first corporate logo, featuring the interlocked initials of its name, seen here on an old gate in the Banda Islands.

Imperial Outposts

The Dutch left many traces of their 350-year stay in the cityscapes of Indonesia, from sturdy churches to elegant bungalows. But they were not the only European colonialists to seek out footings in the archipelago, and long after the region had become the "Dutch East Indies" in the eyes of the outside world there were still isolated outposts of other empires flying foreign flags on far-flung islands.

The Portuguese had been the first European explorers to reach Indonesia and they clung on in a few spots in the east of the archipelago long after their own imperial heyday had passed. In the scattered islands east of Flores, which means "flowers" in Portuguese, and in the one-time hotspots of the spice trade in Maluku, there are crumbling fortifications left by Portuguese sailors.

But the most striking and most poignant imperial relic is at the opposite end of Indonesia, in the remote town of Bengkulu on the wild western coast of Sumatra. For 140 years until 1824 this was one of the remotest, least profitable and most unhealthy fragments of the British Empire. The town is still studded with British monuments and fortifications and the cemetery still holds the haunting memorials of the many soldiers and civilians who never made it home from their bleak postings here.

ABOVE LEFT AND RIGHT The legacy of the long and unhappy British presence in Bengkulu is still writ large in the streetscape of what is now the sleepy capital of a small coastal province. The old part of the town is dominated by the solid ramparts of Fort Marlborough. Built in 1719 in an effort to escape the particularly unhealthy atmosphere of an older—and now largely vanished—fort a short way to the east, it became the base of British operations for the next century before being handed over to the Dutch. Today its ramparts offer fine views, while rusting British cannons still dot the inner courtyard.

THE SPICE OF LIFE

The rattle of a wok over a guttering gas flame, the crackle as a leaf-thin sheet of martabak dough is laid into a pool of hot oil, the sudden sharp scent of lime leaves, and the grainy taste of kopi tubruk, as sweet and dark as a tropical midnight.

Indonesia is a moveable feast, its foods flavored with the heady spice of history. Chinese-style noodles meet Middle Eastern seasonings and Dutch pastries on the counters of Indonesian street stalls, in this, the original home of fusion cuisine. Every region, indeed every decent-sized town, has its own distinctive specialties, from Madura's hearty stews and toothsome sate to delicately grilled seafood in Sulawesi. But thanks to centuries of interisland contact, whether you're looking for lunch in Bandar Aceh or dinner in Kota Ambon, you'll always find an array of offerings from around Indonesia.

Rice, served up in fragrant mounds straight from the steamer, is the bedrock of Indonesian dining, a blank canvas for all manner of accompanying flavors, be that chili-laced *ayam Taliwang*, spatchcocked chicken from West Nusa Tenggara, or dark palm-sugar-sweetened *gudeg*, a jackfruit curry from Yogyakarta.

Bali and Jakarta, cradle of Indonesian tourism and center of urban sophistication respectively, both have high-level restaurant action aplenty, with foreign and local cuisine given fine-dining twists in classy settings. But to truly taste Indonesia, the gourmands of this food-obsessed nation will always tell you, you need to look to the streets. Town centers and sidewalks flanking busy thoroughfares all over Indonesia turn into vast open-air dining rooms at dusk. *Kaki lima* (mobile food carts) and *warung* (simple cafés) with a single specialty are the places to find the finest traditional food. All you need to do is ask for a few local recommendations, or simply keep an eye out for the *warung* with the biggest crowd of diners.

TOP LEFT *Sate*, sometimes also spelt *satay*, is one of the best-known Indonesian dishes, featuring small pieces of skewered meat grilled over charcoal. Within the country it comes in a wide array of different local versions, from *sate Padang* in West Sumatra, served with gloopy curry sauce, to *sate lilit* in Bali, made with minced pork or fish. The best-known variety, however, is *sate Madura*, served with a spicy peanut sauce and hailing from the rocky island that neighbors Java. **MIDDLE LEFT** *Bakso* (meatball and noodle soup) was probably introduced to Indonesia by Chinese traders many centuries ago. The name itself comes from Hokkien Chinese though the dish has become a pan-Indonesian favorite. **LEFT** Indonesia has a rich street food culture. Mobile food carts known as *kaki lima* (meaning "five feet", supposedly after the three wheels of the classic cart plus the two legs of the vendor) ply the streets of every city. Simple tented *warung* (food stalls) line the sidewalks after dark, and market areas, such as this one in Yogyakarta, abound with stalls serving readymade take-away meals to be wrapped up in banana leaves or paper.

TOP The market, *pasar* in Indonesian, is both a place of commerce and a social institution in Indonesia. It's also a vital point of contact between the city and the countryside. Major urban fresh produce markets like that at Kebayoran Lama in Jakarta, seen here in dramatic overview, are served by a constant stream of pickup trucks bringing in fruit and vegetables from outlying areas. Crops such as potatoes, apples and strawberries arrive from the cool fields and orchards of the mountains, while peanuts and tropical fruit come in from the steamy plains.

ABOVE Indonesia's tropical climate produces a wild array of fruits, from instantly familiar bananas and oranges to more outlandish things seldom seen outside the tropics such as *rambutan*, *langsat* and *salak* (also known as snake fruit). Fruit are eaten as snacks but they also serve as ingredients, especially for spicy salads known as *rujak*. The array on display here, including rose apples, cucumbers and unripe mangos, are waiting to be diced and served up dressed with a tangy palm sugar and chili sauce.

ABOVE As in many neighboring countries, chili, on sale here in a Jakarta market along with other culinary essentials, is a central part of Indonesian cuisine. Without it the sauces of Padang cooking would lack their kick, the trademark sweet-spicy mix of Javanese food would be missing, and the fiery element of everything from chicken *Taliwang* to *babi guling* would be absent. But chili is not a native Indonesian ingredient. In fact, it doesn't even belong to the Asian continent. It first arrived only in the sixteenth century in the holds of Spanish and Portuguese ships, which forged a connection between Southeast Asia and South America from where chili originates. Other South American foodstuffs, now ubiquitous in Indonesian kitchens, include papaya, peanuts (a vital Indonesian flavoring) and, of course, potatoes. Quite why the cooks of the archipelago took so readily to these wildly exotic ingredients when they first showed up on the docksides is something of a mystery, though a taste for spicy food was probably already established with the fieriness originally provided by pepper or mustard seeds.

Coffee Plus

At the outer limits of Indonesian cuisine there are some decidedly challenging culinary prospects. The conservation concerned ought to baulk at Bali's black market turtle *sate* and the faint of heart might flee from Makassar's nose-to-tail approach to making beef stew, not to mention the anything-goes attitude to meat eating around Manado at the other end of Sulawesi. But Indonesia's most outlandish food-and-drink creation has somehow achieved legendary status—and legendary price tags—amongst the world's coffee lovers.

The highlands of Java, Sumatra and Sulawesi provide first-class beans for baristas the world over. But the ultimate brew is something a little different. *Kopi luwak*, as it is known, is often described as "the world's most expensive coffee". The inflated price is down to the means of production. To become *kopi luwak* the beans need first to be eaten by a *luwak*, or Asian palm civet, a tree-dwelling weasel-like creature. It's the process of passing through the civet's digestive tract (before being picked out of its droppings at the other end!) that gives *kopi luwak* its superior taste, or so the theory goes. Some serious coffee aficionados dismiss the whole thing as a gimmick.

ABOVE Legend has it that on colonial-era coffee plantations local workers were forbidden from picking the berries for their own use so they took to gathering the bean-filled droppings of wild palm civets instead and stumbled upon uniquely flavorsome coffee. Like so much about *kopi luwak*, however, this may be just a myth.

A plate of food needs a drink to go with it. Liquid refreshment in Indonesia takes in everything from flamboyantly colored concoctions such as *es cendol*, which are half drink, half dessert, to fearsome local moonshines like *brem* and *arak*, brewed in the boondocks of Bali and Lombok, plus, of course, *Bir Bintang*, the ubiquitous local pilsner. But when it comes to identifying a true Indonesian national beverage it's a face-off between coffee and tea.

Of course Java has long been quite literally synonymous with coffee. Since the colonial era both Robusta and Arabica varieties have been grown in the misty uplands here, traditionally served *kopi tubruk* style—a mighty heap of unfiltered grounds and a shovelful of sugar in a glass of boiling water—or perhaps sweetened with a dollop of condensed milk. Tea, though, has the edge when it comes to sheer ubiquity. A tall glass of the stuff, sweetened and served without milk, either hot or chilled with a hunk of ice, is the standard accompaniment for any meal.

OPPOSITE TOP LEFT
Balinese *sate*, on sale here outside the gates of the island's "mother temple", Pura Besakih, is typically made of chicken, pork or fish and served with a spicy chili sauce. It also often comes with a side order of *ketupat*, visible on this stall. These packets, made of woven palm leaves, are filled with sticky rice, then steamed.

OPPOSITE MIDDLE LEFT
The foundation of many Indonesian dishes is a spice paste, generically known as *bumbu*, literally "spice". Most home cooks prepare their own *bumbu*, which typically features chili, garlic and shallots as a base, then various ingredients specific to individual dishes, such as lemongrass, ginger and dried spices. *Bumbu* is traditionally made using a stone pestle and mortar.

OPPOSITE TOP RIGHT *Bakso* is probably the most ubiquitous of all Indonesian street foods. It's a basic meatball soup with fine noodles and clear broth. For many Indonesians it's the ultimate comfort food, a hearty local equivalent to chicken soup. It's also a favorite of Barack Obama, who spent part of his childhood in Jakarta, where he acquired a taste for *bakso*.

ABOVE The diversity of Indonesian cuisine often indicates historical links with far-off lands. In the case of *martabak*, the link is with India. *Martabak* features a paper-thin sheet of dough laid into hot oil then folded around a filling of beaten egg, diced scallions and sometimes chopped meat. It is essentially the same dish as *Mughlai paratha*, served in Bengal.

Padang Food: The National Cuisine

In a place as vast as Indonesia it's little wonder that there are great culinary variations from region to region. But if there's one cooking style that makes a fair claim to being the nationwide favorite, then it has to be the rich, spicy smorgasbord that is *Masakan Padang*, the cuisine of the Minangkabau people of West Sumatra.

There are Padang restaurants in every town in Indonesia. This is multiple-choice dining. A classic Padang-style dinner can feature half a dozen curries, sauces and side dishes. In the most basic Padang eateries you choose the accompaniments for your pile of steamed rice directly from a great stack of dishes up front, but in the classier places an array of as many as twenty small dishes will be brought to your table. At the end you simply pay for those you've dipped into.

The Minangkabau homeland faces onto the western seaboard, and there are touches of spice and heat from India and Arabia in the coconut curries here. There's also fish fried in hot oil, eggplant slow-cooked with chili to a creamy softness and the ultimate Padang dish, *rendang*, a beef or buffalo meat stew cooked for hours over a low heat to become a thick chocolate-colored paste of formidable richness.

ABOVE Padang cuisine features a plethora of different dishes, from spicy curries known as *gulai*, usually with a coconut-based sauce, to crispy fried fish. The basic essentials of a Padang meal, however, are *rendang*, stewed cassava leaves and *balado*, a fiery chili sauce.

MASTERPIECES IN CLOTH, WOOD, METAL AND STONE

Delicate curlicues of dye unfurl across a sheet of creamy silk like forest tendrils. Ghosts of movement flicker through figures, carved into a piece of teakwood in the closest of detail. And fluid limbs reach out from hulks of solid rock. The fine skill of Indonesia's artisans is on full display in the country's varied arts and crafts.

Many centuries have passed since the first stonemason took up his chisel and set about raising a Hindu goddess from a block of basalt, and more centuries still have been and gone since the first weaver bound a fence of tie-dyed threads onto a back-strap loom, but Indonesia's traditional crafts are still going strong. Beyond the piled-high trinkets of the souvenir stalls—and even these often turn out to have a simple artistry of their own—there is a formidable bounty for treasure seekers in the archipelago.

The historical roots of Indonesia's craft of carving in both stone and wood are easy to discern. The bas-relief panels of Borobudur, Prambanan and the dozens of other Hindu-Buddhist temples that stud the Javanese countryside are the ultimate inspirational wellspring for crowded scenes, rendered in the utmost intricacy and so deeply undercut as almost to float free of their backdrops. Today these traditions are continued by the stoneworkers who still live in villages like Tamanagung, close to Borobudur, as well as in the carving communities that flank the southern approach roads to Ubud in Bali. When it comes to the wooden equivalent, meanwhile, the towns of Kudus and Jepara on Java's northern coast ship their fine woodwork around the country.

Indonesia also has a rich artistic heritage in the rather softer medium of cloth. The most famous form of fabric is batik—sheets of silk or cotton subjected to repeated resist-dying, with

RIGHT Batik, one of the best known of Indonesia's cultural contributions to the world, is resist-dyed cloth in which the complex patterns are marked out with wax during the lengthy dying process. The most traditional version is *batik tulis*, literally "written batik", where the patterns are drawn by hand using a *canting*, a small copper bowl with a narrow spout filled with molten wax.

The Hidden Powers of the Kris

The *kris* is the legendary ceremonial dagger of Indonesia, a tapering blade of forged iron with a heavy hilt, an essential element of formal dress in royal Java. But a *kris* is more than a mere weapon or tool. It's a thing heavily laden with symbolism, a physical manifestation of its bearer's masculinity that could even take an aristocratic Javanese man's place on his wedding day should he be detained elsewhere. True heirloom *kris* are also believed to possess potent magical powers, instilled in the blade during the forging process by blacksmiths who double as shamans, and then heightened through the ceremonial care of their owners.

RIGHT The *kris* has been part of Javanese culture for many centuries. Images of *kris*, little different from the current form with the unmistakable wavy, tapering blade, appear in carvings at Borobudur and Prambanan, proof that these blades already existed in the ninth century.

ABOVE *Wayang Kulit* shadow puppetry is first and foremost a performance art. But there is also a high level of craft skill involved in the making of the puppets themselves, cut from sheets of buffalo hide, worked with filigree patterns and then painted in bright colors. Remarkably, the painted decoration remains invisible to a Wayang audience, who see only the silhouette.

OPPOSITE TOP One art form often supports another. Here a skilled woodworker creates intricate carvings, drawing on ancient motifs, to decorate the wooden frames that will support the bronze gongs of a *gamelan* orchestra. In the same workshop in Bogor, West Java, other artisans forge the gongs themselves using traditional methods.

the multilayered patterning sketched out in molten wax. Batik is made in many corners of the archipelago, but Java is its true heartland, with the restrained, convention-bound courtly patterns of the royal cities of Yogyakarta and Solo and the more flamboyant, foreign-influenced motifs of north coast towns like Pekalongan. In the west of the archipelago, in the Malay-speaking heartlands of Sumatra, the dominant fabric form is *songket*, highly complex brocade patterned with threads of silver or gold.

Elsewhere it's metalwork, the making of traditional weapons or musical instruments, the crafting of masks and puppets and the weaving of baskets, all refined and raised to the level of art. Indonesia's painters, meanwhile, take their inspiration from the crowded and stylized scenes on the walls of temples and palaces, while the contemporary innovators whose work hangs in the modern galleries of Ubud and Yogyakarta, the twin poles of Indonesia's art scene, often weave traces of ancient heritage into their twenty-first-century stylings.

All these crafts, though distinctly and inimitably Indonesian, show fine traces of ancient influence from overseas, usually from India or China. Textiles from Nusa Tenggara, for example, often feature *patola* motifs, first introduced to the region in cloth imports from India. But chip away at the layers, and in the deepest recesses you'll find utterly indigenous traditions, the forms sometimes, rather reductively known as "primitive art", though there's nothing remotely primitive about their artistry or their rare power. The Dayak-dominated regions of inner Kalimantan, the remote ancestor-venerating villages of Sumba and several other areas in eastern Indonesia are known for wood carvings intimately connected to traditional belief systems. But it is the Asmat people of swampy lowlands of southwestern Papua who are the true masters of tribal art. Their fabulous carved shields, intricately incised *bis* poles and striking ancestor effigies make for some of the most sought-after traditional art on earth.

Ikat: Picking up the Threads

Though it is overshadowed by batik in the international recognition stakes, Indonesia's other great fabric tradition, *ikat*, is every bit as rich in heritage and woven magic. The word *ikat* simply means "tie" and the key characteristic of this earthy cloth is that its patterning is created by tie-dying of the threads that will make up the warp before they are placed on the loom, a process requiring a remarkably abstract envisioning of the final pattern long before its outline becomes apparent.

The scattered landfalls of East Nusa Tenggara make for the happiest *ikat* hunting ground, with the threads of the traditional cultures of islands like Sumba, Timor and Flores woven into the cloth itself. But *ikat* also turns up in other corners of the archipelago, including Sulawesi and Sumatra. Perhaps the most famous *ikat* of all comes from the village of Tenganan in Bali, where local weavers produce the fabled *gringsing*, a rare "double *ikat*" where the pattern is tie-dyed into both warp and weft in a painstakingly complicated process. The resultant tightly colored cloth is reputed to have supernatural powers.

ABOVE In the *ikat* heartlands of East Nusa Tenggara, each island has its own distinctive weaving style. That from the little island of Rote, seen here on the loom, with the tie-dyed pattern already revealed in the unwoven warp, uses strikingly dark colors.

RHYTHM, RESONANCE, POISE AND MEANING

With perfect poise or earthy abandonment, backed by the multiple melodies of a gamelan ensemble or by nothing more than a rough chant and the stamping of feet, and unfolding on a floodlit stage in a modern concert hall or in the insect-speckled lamplight of a remote village compound, Indonesia's performing arts are as varied as the archipelago itself.

ABOVE *Saman*, originally from the Gayo Highlands of Aceh but now associated with Aceh province in general, is one of Indonesia's most distinctive dances, with the performers on their knees throughout.

From Papuan war dances fit to set your scalp tingling to the rhythmic bobbing and clapping of a row of kneeling Acehnese *Saman* dancers, you'll find distinctive forms of performance from one end of Indonesia to the other. But there's no disputing the fact that the two great linchpins of the performing arts are the courtly capitals of Central Java and the artistic powerhouse that is Bali. These twin hubs share a common point of reference in the culture of the great Hindu-Buddhist kingdoms of old Java. Both often look for narrative inspiration in the Indian epics, the *Ramayana* and the *Mahabharata*, both lace their fiercely complex set-pieces with rich symbolism and ritual significance, and both typically turn to the jangling rhythms of the *gamelan* for a musical backing. But when it comes to delivery, the performances of Java and Bali are as different as the characters of the islands themselves.

Javanese classical dance is closely associated with the royal courts of Yogyakarta and Solo and thus performances here are suffused with the refinement of aristocratic Java. Dances like the *Srimpi* and *Bedhaya* are marked by a delicately subdued *gamelan* rhythm, the usual clattering cacophony of this celebrated Indonesian percussion orchestra somehow toned down to a soothing softness. The performance itself unfolds with a hypnotic aura of control, the dancers seeming to unfurl with all the slow delicacy of a blooming flower—a whispering shuffle of feet, an artfully angled head and the precise flick of a length of silk. Even the battle scenes in the *Wayang Wong*, half dance, half theater and with a fully developed narrative, are delivered with softly stylized precision.

Cross the narrow strait to Bali, meanwhile, and you'll find many of the same basic elements in the island's staggering array of traditional dances. But here the flow of music and movement seems to shift from a trickle to a monsoon spate, the *gamelan* accompaniment coming in a cascade of tumbling scales and the performance itself often loaded with frenetic tension for all its delicacy of gesture and expression.

RIGHT The Sundanese culture of West Java has its own counterpart to the *gamelan* orchestras of the neighboring Javanese heartlands in the form of the *angklung*. Made from lengths of bamboo cut for perfect pitch and suspended to allow maximum resonance, a full *angklung* ensemble creates a unique sound. Here young students at Bandung's renowned Udjo Music School show off their performance skills.

BELOW Many Indonesian dances are more than mere entertainment, serving as important rituals and in some cases supposedly involving supernatural forces. The most famous example of this is Bali's *Barong* dance, in which participants go into a trance and turn their daggers on themselves under the influence of the witch *Rangda* before the spell is broken by the benign lion-like *Barong*.

LEFT Dance forms are not always fixed things. The celebrated *Kecak* of Bali, featuring a scene from the *Ramayana* and a chorus, shown here, who produce a distinctive "chak-chak" chant, has its origins in a 1930s collaboration between expat artist Walter Spies and local dancer Wayan Limbak. Today it is one of Bali's best-known "traditional" dances. **BELOW LEFT** In both Bali and Java a *gamelan* orchestra is an essential accompaniment for important ceremonies. In Bali many villages have their own *gamelan* ensemble made up of volunteer players. In this image, a local from Tejakula on Bali's northern coast plays a xylophone-like *saron* during a temple ceremony. **BELOW** The masked *Topeng* dance is a classic form throughout Java and Bali. Dancers typically draw from the same epic narratives, the *Ramayana*, *Mahabharata* or *Panji* stories, as the *Wayang Kulit*, with their stylized face coverings and manner of movement, instantly recognizable as representations of the key characters to aficionados.

While Yogyakarta and Solo do both have regular scheduled performances, Bali is by far the easiest place to seek out the performing arts, with nightly dance shows by highly skilled troupes in many of the villages around Ubud. Some Balinese dances, like the famous *Kecak* with its chorus of simian chattering, are designed purely for entertainment, but others blur the boundary between performance and ritual, not least the dramatic *Barong*, with its epic battle between good and evil.

The other great Indonesian performing art form, instantly recognizable and thickly wreathed in the fug of fable, is the *Wayang Kulit*. While similar forms of shadow puppetry exist in many other cultures around Asia, nowhere else has it been raised to such levels of complexity and significance. There are local Wayang variants in Bali, Kalimantan and elsewhere, but Java is its true home and it is here that the figure of the *Dalang*, the puppet master, is most potent.

Wayang Kulit features highly stylized puppets made of filigreed buffalo hide (*kulit* means "skin" and *wayang* means "shadow"), manipulated by a single puppeteer against a backlit sheet of cotton with a *gamelan* accompaniment. The stories to be performed are usually drawn from the *Mahabharata* or *Ramayana* and can feature a cast of dozens of separate characters. A full traditional Wayang performance runs without a break, and without the *Dalang* ever leaving his cross-legged position behind the screen, from a few hours after sunset until dawn the following morning, though fortunately there are also much abbreviated versions performed for tourists!

The narratives and formats of the *Wayang Kulit* have been transposed into other forms too: the *Wayang Golok* marionette-style puppet shows of West Java and *Topeng* dances where masked humans take the place of the puppets. They also inform the visual arts, with scenes from the same narratives turning up in paintings and carvings.

Indonesian Pop Music

Travelers are most likely to have *gamelan* or some other traditional form in mind when they think of Indonesian music. But if they end up riding local buses or taxis they're likely to find something very different emerging from the onboard stereo, for this is a country with one of the most varied and vibrant popular music scenes in Asia. Indonesian rock stars and pop princesses are not just celebrities in their own homeland, they also pull big crowds in neighboring Malaysia and Singapore and in other corners of Southeast Asia. Local divas like Agnes Monica massively outsell all their imported American rivals on home turf and soft rock heart throbs like the boys of Noah are met with hordes of screaming fans when they show up onstage.

Indonesia also has sophisticated non-mainstream music movements, ranging from modern folkies wowing the hipsters of Jakarta to ferocious underground punk bands playing in Surabaya dive bars, plus a huge jazz scene. And then there's *Dangdut*, Indonesia's inimitable indigenous pop genre, a musical mélange of Bollywood, Arabia and California with additional local accents which somehow manages to be the Indonesian societal equivalent of Country music!

ABOVE Ivanka, bass player of veteran rockers Slank, Indonesia's answer to the Rolling Stones, doing his thing on stage. **RIGHT** *Dangdut*, Indonesia's indigenous pop-rock tradition that draws on local folk music with added Indian and Arabic influences, typically features lyrics about heartbreak as well as raunchy live performances.

GREAT APES, TIGERS AND DRAGONS

For many travelers the very word "Indonesia" conjures up visions of limitless blankets of tropical forest, rumpled here and there by high ridges, smudged in places with wisps of cottony cloud and stalked by fabulous beasts. And in the wilder parts of the archipelago that's exactly what you get.

Indonesia's wild places range from sun-scorched eastern islets, more reminiscent of African savannah than Southeast Asian tropics, to chilly uplands where a handful of hardy mountain birds find shelter amidst the feathery clumps of Javanese edelweiss. But inevitably it's the jungles that set the tone. Deforestation has taken its toll over the decades, but the two vast landmasses of the western archipelago, Sumatra and Kalimantan, are still amongst the world's greatest rainforest bastions. Sumatra, in particular, as the most southeasterly stronghold of Asian megafauna is a fabled land for those with an eye for wildlife.

Much of Sumatra is formidably remote. The island-long Bukit Barisan mountain range is thickly forested on its lower slopes

and this is where you'll find some of Indonesia's greatest national parks, still home to herds of wild elephants, leopards and an elusive handful of Sumatran rhinos and tigers. None of these creatures are easy to spot, haunting the deepest forests, far beyond roads or even paths. But there's one big forest dweller that's much easier to meet face to face: Asia's only great ape, the long-limbed, rust-colored orangutan. In the delightfully lazy riverside township of Bukit Lawang on the fringes of the enormous Gunung Leuser National Park in the north of Sumatra, these mighty primates are almost always on hand.

Most of Sumatra's other national parks are inaccessible, frontiers for true adventurers. But Way Kambas, down south in

LEFT The orangutan is Indonesia's most iconic wild animal and the only great ape, besides humans, to be found outside of Africa. Two distinct species live in the deep forests of Sumatra, while another species, divided into three recognized subspecies, lives in Borneo.

RIGHT The vast island of Borneo is home to more than a hundred different frog and toad species. Here a pair of tree frogs find a precarious perch near Sambas in West Kalimantan.

FAR RIGHT The Sumatran tiger is the last surviving tiger subspecies in Indonesia (the Bali tiger was hunted to extinction in the 1930s and the Javan tiger is thought to have died out in the late twentieth century). A few hundred wild tigers still live in the remotest parts of Sumatra.

BELOW Known locally as *ora*, the Komodo dragon is the world's largest lizard, growing up to 10 feet (3 meters) in length. They evolved in isolation on the tiny islands of Komodo and Rinca in Nusa Tenggara and are thought to be an example of "island gigantism", where lack of competing large predators allowed monitor lizards to grow to fill a niche usually occupied by big cats and wild dogs elsewhere.

Lampung province, has easy access, good accommodation and the closest thing to a proper safari experience in Indonesia, with elephant encounters a near certainty and a brush with a rhino or a tiger always a tantalizing possibility. There are more huge forest parks across the Java Sea in Kalimantan, with the low-lying swampy levels of Tanjung Puting home to another easily accessible population of orangutans.

Java, with its seething cities and crowded countryside, might not seem like the obvious place to go looking for wilderness. But the island is actually home to some of Indonesia's finest and most beautiful national parks. Ujung Kulon at the westernmost promontory of Java is a World Heritage Site, the last wild refuge of the elusive Javan rhino and also home to all manner of primates and tropical birdlife. There are other lowland parks in East Java too, at Baluran and Alas Purwo. But the bulk of Java's scheduled wildernesses are up amongst the volcanic massifs that run the length of the island. From Gunung Halimun to Bromo-Tengger-Semeru, most visitors come to these places to seek out staggering mountain views rather than wildlife. But the forests that cloak the slopes hold many surprises: a troop of gingery *lutung* monkeys suddenly materializing from the canopy or

even a velvety black leopard glimpsed at first light on a potholed mountain road.

There are other national parks and reserves scattered widely across Indonesia and teeming with their own distinctive wildlife populations. The steamy forests of the West Bali National Park brim with vocal birdlife, while the otherworldly Tangkoko Batuangus Nature Reserve near Manado in northern Sulawesi is home to creatures quite unlike those in the islands further south: crested macaques, hornbills, cucus and the bug-eyed spectral tarsier. But the national park that trumps all others with the iconic inimitability of its resident creatures is made up of a scattering of barren, bony islets rising like knuckles from the turbulent straits between Sumbawa and Flores in Nusa Tenggara. This is the Komodo National Park and here be dragons....

The twin islands of Komodo and Rinca, with their stark landscapes of ribbed, grassy hillsides, along with a couple of smaller neighboring outcrops, plus a few isolated woodlands on the coast of Flores, are the only home of the Komodo dragon, the world's largest monitor lizard. These hulking, carrion-eating monsters, seemingly a Jurassic throwback, can grow up to 10 feet (3 meters) in length, but are easy to see up close on guided visits.

Wallace's Line

Indonesia is divided by the greatest faunal frontier in the natural world, the Rubicon which splits the Asian and Australasian eco-zones and which is known as the Wallace Line. The boundary was first noticed by the pioneering nineteenth-century British naturalist Alfred Russel Wallace, co-conceiver with Charles Darwin of the theory of evolution. Traveling eastwards from Bali to Lombok, a distance of little more than 30 miles (48 km), Wallace noticed a radical change in the resident birdlife, the typically Asian species giving way to the cockatoos and parakeets of the Australian sphere. Bali, it turns out, was the easternmost place ever to have been connected to the Asian mainland during the last Ice Age, while fragments of northeastern Indonesia were originally part of the great southern supercontinent known as Gondwanaland. Modern zoologists recognize that the Wallace Line is less an absolute division than the beginning of a blurry transition zone, which they call Wallacea. But there are still some absolutes: Bali is as far east as big cats have ever lived in the wild, while by the time you reach Papua you start to run into tree kangaroos and other strange marsupials.

RIGHT Sulawesi is the heart of Wallacea, where species from both sides of the notional Wallace Line live side by side. Amongst the primates found here is the tiny bug-eyed spectral tarsier.

LEFT Perhaps the most photogenic of Sulawesi's unique species is the black-crested macaque. These highly social and highly inquisitive monkeys are found only at the northernmost tip of the island, particularly in the Tangkoko Batuangus Nature Reserve, a pocket of pristine coastal rainforest. **ABOVE** Hornbills are among the most striking of all Indonesia's avian residents. There are around half a dozen different species found in the country, with Kalimantan a major hornbill stronghold. The red-knobbed hornbill, pictured here, is found only in Sulawesi. **OPPOSITE TOP** Although it's the big mammals that usually catch the imagination of visitors, the forests of Indonesia are supremely rich with life on a smaller scale. Surveys in Borneo and Sumatra routinely turn up large hauls of new species. Here an elegant tailed green jay, a common species across the region, alights on a flower in Sumatra's Way Kambas National Park.

THE LODESTONE OF THE ARCHIPELAGO

Java punches well above its weight. A lozenge of volcano-studded, temple-speckled land, just 600 miles (965 km) from end to end and 100 miles (160 km) across at its widest point, it is dwarfed by Borneo and Sumatra to the north and west. And yet this is the mighty lodestone of the archipelago, a place of unparalleled contrast and complexity.

Java is home to more than half of Indonesia's entire population and it is where you'll find the country's biggest cities. It has been the stage for the great set-pieces of national history, from the heyday of Hindu-Buddhist culture to the fiery drama of the revolutionary struggle against Dutch colonialism. This past is writ large in Java's landscape. The glass and steel of modern town centers shades into neoclassical masonry in outlying colonial quarters. Palaces ruled by hereditary sultans are stalked by batik-swathed courtiers and thousand-year-old temples still rise from the rice fields.

Java is the natural starting point for a trip through Indonesia, but many foreign visitors arrive primed with preconceptions about this as a hopelessly overcrowded island to be blazed through at speed en route for more distant landfalls. But beyond the big cities Java remains a place of great natural beauty. It is a land where vast volcanoes loiter on the fringes of every journey and where fertility reaches the point of infestation in knotty tangles of trees and creepers. It takes only a few short steps sideways from the major highways to end up in an older, slower-paced world of easy conversation and sweet black coffee.

Happily for travelers, the going in Java is good. The transport infrastructure here is better than anywhere else in the country, and while you won't generally find accommodation matching the stylish sophistication of Bali you certainly won't need to abandon creature comforts. Even well off the beaten tourist track there's generally no need to rough it in Java.

RIGHT Borobudur, the biggest Buddhist monument in the world by some reckonings, is the centerpiece of Java, set in place amidst the supremely fertile, volcano-hemmed countryside that has given rise to many of the island's great historical kingdoms. Its upper levels support 72 individual stupas, each containing a statue of a seated Buddha.

PAGES 36–7 Early morning at 9,800 feet (3,000 meters), hikers pause for rest on the trail around the caldera of Gunung Gede, with the adjoining Pangrango peak visible in the background. This volcano complex towers above Bogor in West Java. It is the most accessible mountain for weekend hiking trips from nearby Jakarta.

RIGHT The walls and balustrades on each of Borobudur's nine lower levels are lined with intricately carved and brilliantly preserved relief panels depicting scenes from Buddhist lore intermingled with glimpses of everyday life in ninth-century Java, some of them still instantly recognizable today. The whole thing amounts to an enormous narrative in stone.

JAKARTA: A TROPICAL MEGALOPOLIS

Swaddled in a blanket of haze and humidity, Indonesia's capital is a city on a colossal scale. Its busy sidewalks are barely a finger's breadth above sea level but the executive lounges of its skyscrapers are halfway to the stars.

Jakarta is home to the country's busiest international airport, so it is the natural port of entry for travelers, many of whom hightail it out of the capital at the first opportunity. But while at first encounter its hugger-mugger mayhem can easily overwhelm, the city has flashes of unexpected charm. As the paramount conurbation of a huge nation striding into the twenty-first century, it has more than its share of cool, from hipster coffee shops to high-flying cocktail lounges. Down at street level, meanwhile, there's an earthy friendliness that puts most other global megacities to shame. And perhaps most importantly for visitors, there is plenty of history riding in the tide of traffic.

The place to begin an urban exploration is the point at which Jakarta itself began, back when it went by the name of Batavia, headquarters of the Dutch East India Company. Fatahillah Square, fronted by the grand old City Hall, is the hub of the area known as Kota, core of the colonial city. There's a bevy of interesting museums here. Further north you'll find the old harbor at Sunda Kelapa, still visited by traditional schooners from far corners of the archipelago, while to the south lie the steamy alleys of Glodok, Jakarta's no-frills Chinatown.

The heart of the modern city lies further south, around the vast park known as Lapangan Merdeka, pinned in place by the slender celebratory tower of Monas, which offers impressive, if hazy, panoramas from its viewing platform. Around the fringes of the park you'll find more museums and grand public architecture. Still further south the world of shopping malls and high-rises takes over, giving way to the long sprawl of the suburbs before the rice fields begin and Java rises towards its mountain core.

ABOVE MIDDLE Towering to 433 feet (132 meters), Jakarta's National Monument, usually abbreviated to Monas, is the city's symbolic center point.

ABOVE Gridlock at dusk. There are an estimated 39 million vehicles, mostly motorbikes, in the Greater Jakarta area, more than there are people!

OPPOSITE TOP Most of Indonesia's cities are dominated by low-rise architecture but Jakarta is a place apart. Since the 1980s the city's developers have reached for the skies and today it is home to over 200 skyscrapers. They flank the major thoroughfares, such as Jalan Thamrin and Jalan Rasuna Said, double ranks of tall towers marching across the cityscape. At the center of this image stands the iconic Wisma 46 building. When it was completed in 1996, shortly before a regional economic crisis that brought a halt to ambitious building projects for several years, it was comfortably the tallest building in Jakarta at 262 meters (860 feet). Today there are three taller towers, with the 948-ft (289-meter) Gama Tower taking top spot.

ABOVE A Jakarta couple are seen here in a moment of private prayer in the huge Istiqlal Mosque, which stands alongside the city's Catholic cathedral to the northeast of the central Merdeka Square. The vast majority of Jakarta residents are Muslims, approximately 86 percent, which is much the same as the national figure. However, as befits a national capital in a diverse country, it is not a particularly conservative place. The Istiqlal Mosque, a striking modernist building opened in 1978, was designed by a Catholic from Sumatra, Frederich Silaban. It can accommodate 200,000 worshippers and is the biggest mosque in Southeast Asia. Outside of prayer times non-Muslim visitors are welcome to tour its huge light-filled halls.

TOP Far from downtown skyscrapers, Fatahillah Square is the heart of old Jakarta. This was the central space of the colonial city known to its Dutch masters as Batavia. The square is dominated by the old *Stadhuis*, or City Hall. The first building to occupy this spot was constructed in 1620. The current grand edifice was erected in 1710 and now serves as the Jakarta History Museum. Local legend has it that the place is haunted. The square itself was once the main market place of Batavia. It was also used for public pronouncements and grim public floggings and executions. Today it has a happier role as a favorite hang-out for both locals and tourists, especially at weekends.

ABOVE Jakarta's Maritime Museum stands in the far north of the city, close to the original harbor area. Even before the first Dutch colonialists arrived, the settlement built at the mouth of the Ciliwung River here was primarily a trading port, known as Sunda Kelapa, a name still used for the working wharf close to the museum. Once the Dutch East India Company arrived it became a major hub for the transshipment of spices from Maluku, rice from Java and all manner of other regional produce, as well as an entry point for trade goods shipped in from Europe. The museum is housed in one of the surviving warehouse complexes from this period, built in the eighteenth century.

INTO WEST JAVA

West Java is, in the Indonesian scheme of things, not really part of Java at all. The island's westernmost provinces are the homeland of the Sundanese people. When locals here speak of "Java" they are talking of a foreign land away to the east.

West Java is overshadowed by Jakarta's looming proximity, but there is much to explore where mountains shoulder up into creamy cloud and southern ridges reach out like knotty green fingers towards the churning Indian Ocean. To the southwest of the capital lies the wilderness of Ujung Kulon, the wild surf of Pulau Panaitan and the ominous reincarnation of the world's most notorious volcano, Krakatau, rising from the tide-swept depths of the Sunda Strait.

The classic West Java journey, however, follows the road or railway due south from Jakarta, up into the cooler air of the mountains. First stop is Bogor, one-time colonial hill station, still dominated by

LEFT ABOVE Bogor's celebrated botanical gardens were founded in 1817 by Casper Reinwardt, commemorated in this monument in the gardens, with the presidential palace, a favorite retreat of Sukarno and still housing his art collection, in the background.

LEFT From Bogor the road to Puncak winds its way ever upwards through the tea gardens that cloak the lower slopes of West Java's mountains. The damp, temperate climate here is perfect for growing tea.

TOP For overheated colonial officials down in the sweltering coastal flatlands, Bandung was once known as *Paris van Java*, "Paris in Java", a supremely sophisticated city with broad boulevards, temperate weather and a lively social scene. Modern Bandung, capital of West Java province, is a busy metropolis, home to 2.5 million people. But its upland setting and mild climate are unchanged and it also has a reputation as a wellspring of talent for Indonesia's pop music industry.

the Kebun Raya botanical gardens, a great green lung at the heart of the town. From Bogor one route strikes south through the hills to the surfers' hangout at Pelabuhan Ratu, but most travelers follow the snaking highway which writhes through the tea gardens to the summit of the Puncak Pass, 4,750 feet (1,220 meters) up on the flanks of the mighty Pangrango and Gede volcanoes, portal to the Priangan Highlands.

Linchpin of these uplands is Bandung, once dubbed "the Paris of the East". Today it is a hectic modern city though it is still surrounded by fine mountain scenery. East of Bandung, road and railway slip through a landscape of overwhelming greenery, high mountains huddling to the north and serried ranks of lower hills stretching southwards towards an empty shoreline, infinitely far removed from the clamor of Bandung and Jakarta. The sleepy beach resort of Pangandaran, real-life inspiration for "Halimunda" in the celebrated novels of Eka Kurniawan, and the nearby surfers' village of Batu Karas are the bases here, places to slow the pace and stare at the horizon before continuing eastwards across an invisible ethnic and linguistic border and into the heart of Java proper.

LEFT Pangandaran under a moody sky. This sleepy seaside town stands in splendid isolation on the wave-lashed southern coast of West Java. Though it's a popular weekend getaway for families from Bandung and other inland towns, it's a quiet place midweek, more a local fishing community than a holiday resort. There are beaches on either side of the town's narrow isthmus where fishermen moor their traditional outrigger boats known as *jukung*.

LEFT ABOVE West Java's answer to the better known *Wayang Kulit* shadow puppetry that has its heartland in neighboring Central Java, is *Wayang Golok*. This performance form draws from the same story cycles as the *Wayang Kulit* but the action is portrayed by marionettes, as seen here in the workshop of a Bandung craftsman. These puppets are worked from below with wooden rods, and a skilled puppeteer can conjure up complex gestures and movements.

Krakatau: The Big Bang

It's a name that resounds down the centuries: Krakatau, ultimate synonym for volcanic catastrophe. In 1883 this island volcano, a dark and lonely sentinel in the middle of the strait which separates Java from Sumatra, blew itself to pieces in a single monumental explosion, killing some 36,000 people, sending tsunamis sweeping across surrounding shorelines and darkening the sky for days to come.

You can visit the site of this biggest of bangs by boat from the beach resort of Carita on the western coast of Java. Though Krakatau itself was destroyed by the eruption, fragments of the caldera remain as well as the new island volcano known as Anak Krakatau, "Child of Krakatau", which has been slowly rising out of the depths since 1927.

Anak Krakatau is a menacing presence in the Sunda Strait. It is possible to get up close to the island by boat from Carita. When the volcano is quiet it's even possible to go ashore and climb to the summit though it is often dramatically active, as in this striking image.

THE CENTRAL JAVANESE HEARTLAND

The southern volcanic plains of Central Java are the wellspring of Javanese culture. It is here that the traditional arts, from classical dance to batik, are at their most refined. It is also here that the hierarchy-bound Javanese language is at its most refined, and it is here that fantastical history is layered most thickly.

The hub of the region is Yogyakarta. Uniquely in republican Indonesia, this most Javanese of cities is still the seat of a reigning sultan with officially acknowledged status, a legacy of the ninth sultan's support for the Independence movement during the 1940s. The heart of the town is still the Kraton, the royal palace built on the classic Javanese model, with its network of shady courtyards and airy pavilions. Yogyakarta is not all about time-honored tradition, however. It's also Indonesia's ultimate student city, sizzling with contemporary creativity.

Thirty miles (48 km) up the road, Solo, also known as Surakarta, has long since gotten used to playing second fiddle to Yogyakarta, though it is, in fact, the older courtly center. This was the seat of the mighty Mataram kingdom before it was partitioned in the mid-eighteenth century, and for savvy travelers Solo is a place that has most of the attractions of Yogyakarta,

TOP The Kraton of Yogyakarta is still bound by an extremely complex system of courtly tradition and protocol. The Kraton is attended by a large retinue of *abdi dalem* (courtiers), both male and female. The minutely graded rank and status of these courtiers can be determined by variations in their formal Javanese dress.

ABOVE Within the walls that hem the inner quarters of Yogyakarta is the Taman Sari, the so-called "water palace". Built by the first sultan, Mangkubumi, in the late eighteenth century, this was once a profoundly private place, with bathing pools for the women of the royal household and a series of secretive underground tunnels and chambers.

RIGHT Though it is overshadowed by nearby Yogyakarta, Solo has the stronger pedigree as a royal city. The court here lost its official statues after Indonesian independence but it is still a powerful institution, presided over by a hereditary *Susuhunan*. Here a royal parade passes through the city with appropriate pomp and circumstance.

including a fascinating *kraton*, or palace, and a vibrant batik and crafts industry, but far fewer sightseeing crowds.

To the north of Yogyakarta, Solo and the temples of Borobudur and Prambanan, lies an arc of gargantuan volcanic peaks. The Dieng Plateau, more than 6,000 feet (1,830 meters) up in the cool air above the mountain town of Wonosobo, is the centerpiece of the mountains, a strange round of level land in the belly of an old volcano, speckled with some of the oldest temples in Java. Further east, the Sumbing, Sindoro, Merbabu and Merapi volcanoes are mighty giants, while Gunung Lawu, rising to the east of Solo, is a mountain steeped in historical and mystical significance, with unearthly temples from the dying days of Majapahit perched on its high flanks and a few isolated mountain communities which still maintain a Hindu identity in Muslim-majority Java.

LEFT ABOVE The Dieng Plateau is a beautiful upland area, with colored lakes tinged by volcanic deposits and fine views of the huge surrounding mountains, such as the conical Sindoro and the more distant Merbabu seen in the background here. But it is also a place of considerable historical significance. The plateau, itself the crater of an ancient volcano, is dotted with Hindu temples, most dating from the eighth century. These are amongst the oldest temples in Java, and though they are relatively small in stature they prefigure the epic temple-building traditions which would unfold on the nearby plains in the centuries that followed.

LEFT Solo has a long history as a center of the cloth industry. Indeed, some of the early stirrings of Indonesian nationalism arose out of organizations originally founded here as unions of cloth merchants.

Prambanan and Borobudur: Temple Treasures

Rising in mountains of intricately incised volcanic stone to tower over the surrounding thickets of palms and banyans, Prambanan and Borobudur, the great temples of Central Java, are amongst Indonesia's most celebrated attractions. Dating from the late centuries of the first millennium CE, they represent the crowning glory of classical Java's artistic tradition, miracles to rank with the other wonders of the world, such as the Taj Mahal and Angkor Wat.

Borobudur, a vast multi-tiered pyramid, each level lined with bas-relief friezes from Buddhist lore, is the older of the duo, built over the course of seven decades between the eighth and ninth centuries. Its gray andesite hulk still dominates a natural amphitheater of hills. Prambanan, in contrast, was built in a very different style in the century that followed. Black basalt is the medium here, Shaivite Hinduism is the religious focus, and an ensemble of slender, skyscraping towers is the form, every level thickly crusted with friezes and statuary, a little pocked and weathered after 1,100 monsoons but still full of detail and dynamism.

Prambanan lies a short way beyond the eastern suburbs of Yogyakarta, just off the main road to Solo, and it's easily visited as a day trip from either city. Borobudur is a little further afield, in the hills south of Magelang. It's also easily visited as a day trip from Yogyakarta, but to really soak up a sense of the place after the crowds have gone home it's well worth staying the night in the adjoining village.

ABOVE The 72 stupas that top Borobudur each contains a seated Buddha statue. Some stupas have lost their outer shells over the centuries, leaving the Buddha fully uncovered. **RIGHT** Seen from above the grand design of Borobudur is revealed: a vast mandala, a symbolic representation of the cosmos. **BELOW** Sky lanterns drift over Borobudur on the night of *Waisak*, a major Buddhist festival. After a thousand years of abandonment, the temple began to attract new Buddhist communities in the twentieth century.

A NORTH COAST JOURNEY

Most travelers in Java follow the southern route between Bandung and Yogyakarta, winding from high mountains to stormy shorelines and weaving past pockmarked temples. But there is an alternative. Along the northern littoral, a region known as the *Pasisir*, you'll find another side of Java. This was Java's point of contact with the world for thousands of years. In the towns of the Pasisir, strung like rough gemstones on the thread of the main Jakarta-Surabaya highway, there are bowed rooflines, steaming noodles and flashes of scarlet to flag up a Chinese influence. There are mounds of sticky dates and a faint scent of cumin, speaking of ancestries in the Hadhramaut region of Arabia. There are saints' graves rising from the myth-wreathed subsoil of early Javanese Islam. There are voices speaking of Malaysia and Madura and Makassar, as much as of Majapahit or Mataram. And behind the workaday modern bustle there is a wealth of mildewed Dutch architecture.

Heading eastwards, Cirebon is the first coastal town of note, an ancient court center with a trio of *kratons*, places of faded grandeur, cobwebby corners and Dutch-style tilework. Further

TOP Cultural continuities are revealed in the unusual architecture of the *Masjid Menara*, the "Tower Mosque" at the heart of Kudus, a small town east of Semarang. Originally built in the sixteenth century, it is one of the oldest mosques in Java. Its tower, in both multi-tiered form and red-brick material, closely echoes the temple-building traditions of Majapahit, the last great Hindu-Buddhist kingdom to rule in Java before Islam became the main religion.

RIGHT ABOVE Semarang is home to many atmospheric Chinese temples, such as Tay Kak Sie, shown here. Dating from 1772, the main deity worshipped here is the Goddess of Mercy. In front of the temple is a modern statue of Zheng He, also known as Cheng Ho, a Chinese admiral who commanded a huge Chinese fleet that visited Java in 1407. Zheng He was actually a Muslim but he is venerated by Southeast Asia's Chinese communities.

on, Pekalongan is a modest little town with a lively batik industry. The highway hereabouts spars with the soft shoreline of the Java Sea, spanning muddy inlets crowded with candy-colored fishing boats. To the south the high mountains rise into plum-dark cloud.

Fulcrum of the Pasisir is the great trading city of Semarang. Crowded up against its writhing riverbanks there are sprawling historical quarters, places of steamy alleys plied by rattletrap pedicabs, Chinese temples with dragon-chased rooftops and barnlike Dutch warehouses. But perhaps the most interesting slice of the whole Pasisir lies to the east of Semarang, around the flanks of Gunung Muria, isolated outrider of Java's volcano legion. This was the antechamber of Islam in the island, the point at which Muslim culture first met and mixed with older Hindu-Buddhist traditions, and in the towns of Kudus, Demak and Jepara there is still a lingering sense of cultural fusion. Jepara is also a handy hopping-off point for voyages to Karimunjawa, an archipelago of 27 coral-ringed islets, a world away from the Pasisir's truck-plied highways.

The Gedong Songo Temples

As the livid stain of the coming day spreads across the eastern skyline a quartet of mighty mountains form from the murk: the warty hulk of Merbabu, with Merapi's belligerent summit peeking over its shoulder and the neat triangles of Sumbing and Sindoro closer at hand. Down below a galaxy of village lights still shows beneath a creeping tide of milky mist, and the dull mirror of the Rawa Pening Lake is just beginning to reflect the paling sky.

Perched on the slopes of Mount Ungaran, south of Semarang, the eighth-century Gedong Songo temples might not match Borobudur and Prambanan when it comes to scale but they surely take the top spot when it comes to their early morning outlook. Though they get busy with trippers from Semarang at weekends, on a weekday morning you'll often have the temples to yourself. The old-fashioned hill resort of Bandungan, further down the mountainside, makes for a pleasantly cool overnight stop.

LEFT Fishing is still an important industry along the north coast of Java and huge fleets of open boats set sail each evening to work in the sheltered waters of the Java Sea. The boats that dock at Jepara are often beautifully decorated. **ABOVE** Unlike in Yogyakarta and Solo where tradition-bound Javanese abstract patterns dominate the cloth industry, the batik makers of Cirebon and other north coast centers use floral motifs and other design elements influenced by long maritime connections with China and Europe.

ABOVE The name Gedong Songo means "Nine Buildings" in Javanese, though in fact there are just six separate temple groups scattered amongst the pine trees at around 4,000 feet (1,200 meters) above sea level. The name was first recorded by Dutch surveyors, though the place was actually known by locals as *Candi Banyukuning*, the "Yellow Water Temples", evoking the sulfurous hot springs that bubble out of a nearby hillside. The temples were built in the eighth century, making them some of the oldest in Java.

ACROSS THE MOUNTAINS: INTO EAST JAVA

There are several routes into East Java. Southeast from Yogyakarta a lonely highway blazes through empty karst landscapes to the waning moon of pale sand at Pacitan, a frontier for pioneering surfers. To the north, meanwhile, the main road to Surabaya slips across the seamless provincial border between Sragen and Ngawi with green in all directions. But the most dramatic portal to the east is the mountain road from Solo, up through the pine trees of Tawangmangu and across a breezy pass on the flanks of Gunung Lawu.

From here an excellent southern route through East Java follows the fringes of the main mountain chain. There is little of the heavy traffic that plies the northern coastal route here and for long stretches between the towns there is nothing but forest and rice fields, dotted here and there with red-roofed hamlets and bone-white mosques. Blitar, with its enduring atmosphere of old-world Java, is the most interesting settlement hereabouts. This is where Sukarno, Indonesia's first president, spent much of his childhood. North of the town, knee deep in the rice and pineapple fields, is the Panataran temple.

The centerpoint of the East Java hinterlands is Malang, nestled in the bowl of level land between the vast Bromo-Tengger and Arjuno-Welirang volcano massifs. Once a Dutch hill station, today it is a bustling upland city full of students and day-trippers from the overheated coast. But it still has its fair share of colonial atmosphere amongst the villa-lined back streets and it is still ringed by a broken halo of thirteenth-century temples.

From Malang a busy highway descends on a gentle bearing to Surabaya, an incongruous metropolis in this wildest of Javanese provinces. As Indonesia's second biggest city it has high-end shopping and accommodation aplenty, but it also has sprawling historical quarters, left over from the days when Surabaya was the biggest port of the Dutch East Indies, mentioned in the same breath as Hong Kong, Shanghai and Singapore. These northern neighborhoods, away from the malls and multiplexes, are full of smoke-darkened Chinese temples, crumbling shop-houses and covered markets where splintered sunlight falls through clouds of garlic-scented dust.

TOP LEFT East Java is a province dominated by high mountains. A chain of volcanic massifs rising to around 10,000 feet (3,000 meters) runs east to west from Gunung Lawu on the border with Central Java to the Ijen complex looming over the Bali Strait. The upper levels of these mountains are clad with pine forests, and nighttime temperatures can be very chilly indeed. Here the morning mist begins to dissipate over the ridges at Sukapura on the slopes of the huge Bromo-Tengger massif.

ABOVE Surabaya's Masjid Al Akbar, better known as Masjid Agung, is a masterpiece of modern Islamic architecture. Work began in 1995, and though the regional economic crisis of the late 1990s stalled the project it was completed in 2000. It draws on elements from Central Asian, Turkish and Javanese traditions. The central dome and turquoise mosaic work echo Persian styles and the free-standing minaret is built along Ottoman lines. But the pyramidal roofs over the secondary halls are a purely Javanese element.

Madura: An Island Apart

The long, low island of Madura rides off the north coast of Java like a ship at anchor, tethered to the mainland at Surabaya by a slender thread of concrete and steel. This craggy sliver of limestone has long had a testy relationship with its bigger neighbor to the south and even today many Javanese people are quick to badmouth Madura, without having ever visited themselves. But don't listen to the stories of heat, dirt and singularly rough and ready people, for in truth Madura is a fascinating off-the-beaten track adventure where the welcome is as warm as anywhere in Indonesia.

Thanks to the building of Indonesia's longest suspension bridge, known as "Suramadu", it's now easy to skip over the 3-mile (5-km) channel from Surabaya. The most interesting part of Madura, however, lies at the eastern end of the island, around the sleepy one-time royal capital of Sumenep. The countryside around here has quiet lanes leading to long sweeps of empty sand or pretty fishing harbors on narrow inlets.

Madura is famous for two things: its succulent *sate* (barbecued skewers, usually of lamb or goat meat) and its high-octane bull racing, which takes place in the late dry season in towns all over the island.

ABOVE Until 2009 the only way to reach Madura was by sea. But then the ambitious Suramadu (short for Surabaya-Madura) bridge was opened, stitching mainland Java directly to its near neighbor for the first time. The bridge is over 3 miles (5 km) long and is a worthy attraction in its own right, especially when dramatically lit up at night.

ABOVE Java is not known for its beaches. But hidden behind deep ranges of coastal hills and sheltered by headlands of craggy limestone, the entire south coast is dotted with pockets of golden sand. Some of the most accessible are to be found around Pacitan, a pleasant seaside town close to the provincial border with Central Java. Srau Beach, seen here, is a short way west of the town. Like many spots in this area it is popular with surfers, and small accommodations and restaurants have spring up to service them.

TOP In 2017 a village near Semarang found fame after locals gave it a colorful makeover. The idea has since caught on and a second "rainbow village" has appeared in the upland town of Malang, which sits in a bowl of elevated land between major volcano complexes. The riverside Jodipan area shown here was once the most run-down part of Malang until community activists and local students got to work with colored paint. It now attracts a steady stream of camera-toting visitors.

THE WILD EAST: JAVA'S OUTER LIMITS

The extreme east of Java has always been a land apart, far from the courtly cities of Yogyakarta and Solo and further still from Jakarta. Beyond Surabaya the island narrows into a slender promontory. This was the last part of Java to convert to Islam. Indeed, up in the chilly mists around the Bromo-Tengger Massif, they never joined the new religion at all. Even closer to sea level, amongst the concertinaed rice terraces, syncretic traditions still linger. Mountains dominate the landscape and the imagination here: Semeru, Argopuro, Raung and an army of outliers. This is one of the most dramatic regions of Java to travel through.

Centerpiece of this wild mountain country is the vast Bromo-Tengger caldera, surely the most photographed panorama in Indonesia, with its unmistakable alignment of ribbed volcanic cones and its vast sunken sea of sand, all surmounted by Semeru, Java's highest and most sacred summit. But there are other accessible uplands too, not least Ijen, Java's final mountain bastion before the narrow strait that leads to Bali, with its coffee plantations, velvety dark nights and legendary tough sulfur miners.

The far east of Java also has some of the island's wildest national parks. This was the last haunt of the Java tiger, and though this stately cat is almost certainly now extinct there are just enough rumors and unconfirmed sightings to keep a faint frisson of possibility alive out there in the jungle. The Meru Betiri National Park, stretching south of Jember, is a true wilderness and hard to reach, though the protected turtle beach at Sukamade has both access and accommodation. Further east, Java's final promontory, Alas Purwo, has forest trails and world-famous surf at Grajagan, also known as G-Land. But the prime wildlife-watching destination in all of Java lies at the island's northeastern corner, at Baluran, where unexpected expanses of open grassland amidst a patchwork of forest make it easy to spot the herds of deer, *banteng* and wild buffalo that thrive here. And there's always the thrilling chance of catching a glimpse of a leopard moving through the undergrowth like a living pool of sunlight and shadow.

FAR LEFT The base of the huge Bromo caldera is known as the *Lautan Pasir*, the "Sea of Sand", thanks to its thick carpet of gray volcanic sand. Visitors can traverse this eerie landscape on foot, by jeep or on horseback.

LEFT The sulfur miners of Ijen have one of the toughest jobs in Indonesia. Around 400 men from villages on the lower slopes descend into the crater here each day to harvest sulfur deposits with only basic tools and protection. They carry loads of around 200 pounds (90 kg) twice a day along the steep path from the base of the crater and then down to a weighing station in the forest below. The sulfur is used in pharmaceuticals and the sugar industry.

ABOVE The dawn view of the Bromo caldera from the Penanjakan viewpoint, seen here, is an essential image of Java. Bromo itself is just a small part of this epic panorama—the smoking crater seen at the back of the inner caldera. In front of it are the ribbed slopes of Batok, a second, currently dormant inner peak, while in the far distance rises Semeru, the highest and most sacred mountain in Java, at over 12,000 feet (3,676 meters).

RIGHT East Java's southern shores are relentlessly battered by the powerful swells of the Indian Ocean, and the whole coast is dotted with excellent surf spots, from G-Land in the east to Watu Karang, seen here, in the west.

THE ISLAND OF THE GODS

Bali stands out. A rough rhomboid of land set halfway along the narrowing belt of islands that stretches all the way from Sumatra to Papua, it is one of Indonesia's smallest provinces, yet it looms large in the world's imagination. For millions of travelers each year Bali is the go-to island getaway, but despite the crowds it retains a powerful magic in its dark hinterland.

Bali is a compact space, small enough to circuit in a single long day. But at the same time it is so densely packed with variety that you could spend weeks on the road here, skipping from seething southern resorts to ravine-side hideaways to misty mountain villages to quiet coral shorelines and beyond, ever onwards.

The island has been able to withstand the onslaught of mass tourism for several reasons. For a start, the full-bore development has largely been restricted to the far south, close to the airport. Secondly, the island has bone structure to die for: mountains, ridges and rice terraces assembled into a landscape that can stop you in your tracks at each bend of an upland road. And most importantly of all, there's the island's distinctive culture. Bali is unique within Indonesia as the only region to have been subjected to the full force of Indian-influenced Hindu-Buddhist culture in centuries past, but not subsequently to have converted to Islam. Today the distinctive Hindu-Bali traditions still give the place its color, like a thread of fine gold thread woven into a backcloth of the deepest green.

Because of its small size, virtually every corner of Bali can be visited as a day trip whatever your point of departure. But it is always worth shifting bases at least a few times during a stay to properly absorb the sheer variety of this paramount island.

RIGHT Bali is dominated, physically and spiritually, by the mighty Gunung Agung volcano. Rising to 9,994 feet (3,031 meters) at the center of the island, it is the most sacred summit for Balinese Hindus and the point towards which temples and family compounds are orientated. The streams that spring from its slopes, meanwhile, provide irrigation for agriculture in the surrounding areas, such as Sideman, shown here.

RIGHT The *Barong*, portrayed here in a performance in Ubud, is a benign force in Balinese mythology, doing battle with the evil witch *Rangda*. In its current form the *Barong* clearly borrows from the Chinese lion dance but the figure itself probably draws on ancient indigenous traditions.

LEFT Seminyak, towards the northern end of Bali's west coast strip, is the most sophisticated beach town on the island, with boutiques, high-end restaurants and magnificent sunsets.
BELOW LEFT With little level ground to spare, Bali's airport was built on reclaimed land at the island's narrow southern isthmus. It makes for spectacular views on landing.
BELOW Seminyak was once nothing more than a fishing hamlet. These days it's one of Asia's most desirable destinations, home to high-end art galleries, such as the one shown here.

MAXIMUM BALI: THE BUSY SOUTH

As the plane banks in for arrival at Bali's Ngurah Rai International Airport, wedged like a splinter in the island's narrow southern isthmus, there are glimpses of what lies beyond: long lines of surf unfurling over shallow reefs, red roofs rising from a thicket of palms and, if you're lucky, a brief vision of a vast mountain looming out of plum-dark cloud. Once you're out of the airport terminal there's little to cushion the impact. This is Bali at its modern maximum, with roaring roadways and brash commercialism at every turn. But even here there are little flashes to show that this is no ordinary holiday island: a glimpse of an ornate temple amongst the restaurants, the image of a woman in a lacy *kebaya* bending to place an offering on the threshold of a gift shop, and a whiff of incense tempering the heat and dust.

Southern Bali is where tourism first took hold in the 1970s and the coast here, fanning out on either side of the provincial capital,

OPPOSITE BOTTOM Kuta is Bali's original surf city. The first person ever to ride a wave here was probably American hotelier Bob Koke in the 1930s. But it was in the 1970s that things really took off as young Australians arrived and locals quickly followed their lead.

BELOW Bali's unique atmosphere derives from the fact that ritual life goes on undiminished in the middle of even the busiest tourist areas. Here local women in Seminyak take part in the Melasti purification ritual, which is held at the edge of the sea in mid-March.

Surfing in Bali

Bali means many things to many people but to the world's surfers the island's name evokes one thing only: endless waves delivered up with unswerving consistency by the deep storm systems of the Southern Ocean then crafted to glassy perfection over craggy coral reefs by soft jasmine-scented land breezes. Since the early 1970s wave-riders from California to Cornwall have dreamed of Bali and they still come lugging their padded board bags through the gates of the airport terminal in their thousands each year.

The mainstay of Balinese surfing is the Bukit Peninsula. The string of celebrated breaks at the foot of the cliffs here are the stuff of legend in surfing circles, especially the mighty Uluwatu and the fearsome Padang-Padang. This is where the prime surf action is to be found in the dry season. During the wet months, when wind and swell directions flip, the focus shifts to the eastern shore, from Nusa Dua through Serangan and Sanur to Keramas and a few secret points further up the coast where in-the-know foreigners trade perfect right-hand barrels with local hotshots. For those less steady on their feet, however, the best place to take to the waters is Kuta Beach.

ABOVE The spot known to international wave-riders as Uluwatu after the nearby temple and to locals by its original name, Suluban, is the mainstay of the island's surf scene, shown here. Close to the southernmost tip of the Bukit Peninsula, it catches the maximum swell during the dry season, and with waves unfolding through several peaks along a huge stretch of reef it can accommodate large crowds.

LEFT A priest blesses the site of a sacred dance performance in Denpasar. Many entertaining dances double as important rituals.
RIGHT The Uluwatu temple complex is the most spectacular dance venue in Bali, where the *Kecak* "monkey" dance is performed each evening.
BELOW The craggy coast of the Bukit Peninsula has sprouted many boutique hotels in recent years, such as this one, south of Jimbaran.
BOTTOM The stretch of beach that runs from Kuta north to Seminyak is a huge space, with room for horse riding at low tide.
OPPOSITE BOTTOM Towards sunset the beach at Jimbaran turns into a huge open-air seafood restaurant.

Denpasar, is lined with resort districts. On the west coast Kuta is a boisterous low-budget party town which shades northwards via Legian into Seminyak's high-flying sophistication, while on the opposite eastern shore Sanur has a calmer seaside charm and Nusa Dua is a gated complex of high-end luxury and air-brushed beaches. South of all this is one of Bali's most distinctive areas, a slab of limestone known as the Bukit Peninsula. For years this was an outland avoided by all but a few impoverished subsistence farmers. Today it is home to many classy villa hideaways, but a certain wildness still endures, not least at the foot of the high cliffs where Bali's finest surfing conditions are to be found.

Those who come seeking "the real Bali" sometimes find the busy south is too much: too much traffic, too many people, too little open space. But it does have supreme shopping, dining and accommodation. It's also easy to get away on day trips. And, of course, there's always the ocean, sizzling onto the pale sand beneath a Seminyak sunset or lapping the Sanur shoreline in the lavender light of dawn.

Nusa Lembongan and Nusa Penida: Islands Out of Time

Stand on the beach at Sanur and you'll see it: a bank of land rising out of the waters 10 miles (16 km) to the east. Its ribbed escarpment looks almost close enough to touch but also impossibly distant—a prospect to fire the imagination.

In fact, this Balinese outrider is not a single landmass. It is a trio of islands: Nusa Lembongan closest to shore, tiny Nusa Ceningan hunkered behind it and the far bigger hulk of Nusa Penida rising beyond. Nusa Lembongan has been an offshore playground for surfers, divers and sunset-gazers for years. Its western shore is lined with resorts and guest houses though an absence of land traffic keeps the castaway atmosphere intact. But to truly step beyond the beaten track you'll need to go further, to Nusa Penida.

The phrase "like Bali thirty years ago" is much overused, but when it comes to Nusa Penida it might just be apt. Until very, very recently this entire island, with its craggy southern cliffs sheltering hidden white beaches and its potholed backroads winding through empty hill country, was virtually unvisited by tourists. Today it is slowly opening up, with a smattering of decent accommodation options appearing around the village of Ped in the north and in the hills behind the beautiful Crystal Bay beach in the west, but it still feels like an island out of time.

A rickety vehicle ferry runs most days from Padangbai to the scruffy main town of Sampalan, while smaller, faster boats from Benoa and Sanur streak across the channel to Ped and Toyapakeh. Once ashore you'll find that a rented motorbike or a chartered minibus is the best way to explore. You'll meet more chickens on the roads here than fellow drivers. There are some striking sights on Nusa Penida, not least the cave temple at Goa Giri Putri where a tiny aperture opens into a vast sacred cavern. But the island's greatest attraction is simply its air of isolation, a slab of lonely land drifting out of time yet in view of the busy beaches at Sanur.

ABOVE Goa Giri Putri is an unearthly underworld and a major highlight of a visit to Nusa Penida. Set inside a huge natural limestone cavern accessed via a narrow passageway, this sacred site features numerous shrines and an atmosphere thick with the scent of incense.

UBUD AND BEYOND:
HEADING FOR THE HILLS

As far as many aficionados are concerned, the real Bali begins along the road that rolls northwards and gently uphill through Batubulan at the northeast corner of Denpasar. Someone seems to have fiddled with the thermostat hereabouts as the baking heat of the beaches dials down a notch and on an overcast morning there's even an illusion of proper cool. The minimarts and fast food joints give way to craft workshops with great gray armies of carved Buddhas impassively peering out at the traffic. And here and there, between the buildings, comes an emerald flash, a rice field and a wall of impenetrable greenery.

Ubud sits pretty in the midst of all this. It might have swollen out of all proportion since the first international bohemians set up camp here in the 1920s and 1930s, and in doing so helped to forge the enduring vision of Bali as an earthly paradise for artistically inclined expats. But while its detractors sometimes proclaim modern Ubud a paradise lost, little more than an overcrowded *Eat, Pray, Love* theme park, there's no doubt that this is still a tourist town like no other. Whether your budget limits you to a simple guest room in a family compound or stretches to a stay in an ultra-exclusive spa resort, the whole place comes suffused with "Bali Style". There's imaginative dining, art at every turn and the most accessible traditional dance and music performances anywhere in Indonesia. And though tour buses and motorbikes clog the center of town, there's still a strong sense of a local Balinese community interlocking easily with the modern tourist industry.

What's more, Ubud is surrounded by some of Bali's most beautiful and culturally rich landscapes. This region, around the catchments of the fast-flowing streams that streak southwards from the central mountains, was the original cradle of Balinese culture. The vein-like web of country roads that fans out from Ubud leads to all manner of ancient temples and archeological sites as well as to terraced gorges and quiet villages. And just a little further afield, north of Tabanan, say, there are miles and miles of pristine countryside where the idea that Bail is somehow "spoiled" is quickly overturned.

LEFT TOP A young Balinese dancer strikes a pose in full *Baris* costume. The *Baris* is performed by men. It depicts a warrior readying for battle. The word *Baris* itself originally referred to a formation of soldiers from the courts of Bali. During the dance the performer's movements become progressively more confident until he assumes the persona of an unassailable hero. As well as the solo performance there are ritual versions of the dance, such as the *Baris Gede* that features ranks of armed dancers.

LEFT MIDDLE At the heart of Ubud is a large market where the contemporary tourist town and the traditional agricultural center come together in a warren of stalls and hole-in-the-wall shops. Known locally as *Pasar Seni*, which means simply "art market", the place is jam-packed with cheap handicrafts and souvenirs. But this is also the original shopping venue for Ubud locals, the place to go for fresh produce and household items. In the lower levels it is a colorful traditional market.

OPPOSITE BOTTOM Dancing is a respectable career in Bali and the rise of tourism has meant that there is always work for dance troupes. Children see their first dances at an early age and those who enter training, such as these girls in Ubud, are already long familiar with the routines. Training begins, as here, with rows of novices following a teacher's lead. This later gives way to intense one-on-one sessions where the teacher guides the trainee's limbs through each intricate movement.

ABOVE In the 1920s Ubud was a sleepy village and minor royal center. Then the first artistically inclined expats turned up, led by the German painter Walter Spies, and the place quickly developed a reputation as a kind of paradise. This reputation endured through the political upheavals of the mid-twentieth century, and in independent Indonesia the place continued to grow, eventually becoming the New Age metropolis of galleries, retreats and excellent organic restaurants, such as the one shown here, that it is today.

ABOVE The tranquil Pura Taman Saraswati shown here stands in the heart of Ubud. Dedicated to Saraswati, the Goddess of Learning, the building was designed in the 1950s by I Gusti Nyoman Lempad, one of the most celebrated of all Balinese artists. Lempad designed many of the temples and palaces around Ubud and also produced delicate inked images on paper. Although his exact birthdate was never clear, he was certainly well over 100 years old by the time he died in 1978.

TOP Tegallalang, a short way north of Ubud, is famed for its rice terrace views. The steep valley here has been intricately worked over the centuries, with every inch of ground taken up by narrow rice plots following the natural contours. Easily viewable from the road, it attracts plenty of visitors, especially at sunset. In truth, this is just one small fragment of Bali's spectacular agricultural landscape and there are equally impressive terraces in many other places around the island.

INTO THE EAST

Before the Dutch finally gained outright control of Bali in the early years of the twentieth century, a process of conquest which involved appalling bloodshed, the island was divided between eight sporadically feuding fiefdoms. Today the outlines of these erstwhile independent kingdoms still survive as the borders of Bali's regencies, the units of local government below that of province. The two easternmost kingdoms—pint-sized Klungkung and mighty Karangasem—were once Bali's most powerful states. Today, though, they are quiet backwaters where an old-time atmosphere endures and where the world of villas and boutiques and spas vanishes like morning mist.

A smooth modern coastal highway streaks northeastwards from Denpasar, but the further you travel along it the thinner the flow of traffic becomes, and by the time you reach its terminus close to the fishing village of Kusamba and return to an older two-lane road there's a sense of having stepped back a decade or two into a gentler, slower-paced Bali. A left turn here leads to Klungklung town, the one-time royal capital, and beyond to the sublime valley of Sideman. Most travelers, however, turn right into Karengasem, a wilder, emptier region dominated by the rearing form of Gunung Agung, fulcrum of the Balinese universe.

ABOVE These days Karangasem, Bali's easternmost regency, is something of a sleepy backwater far removed from the hectic population centers of the south. But this was once one of the most powerful of all Bali's feuding kingdoms. The last independent ruler of Karangasem, Gusti Bagus Djelantik, commissioned a series of beautiful "water palaces" around his kingdom in the early twentieth century. That at Ujung, pictured here, is the most extensive, an elegant fusion of European and Balinese styles near the coast south of Amlapura.

BELOW At the heart of Klungkung, now a modest market town in eastern Bali, is the *Kerta Gosa*. This "hall of justice" stands in the grounds of the Klungkung royal palace. It is an open-sided pavilion built alongside a pool and it was the place where the raja and his attendant priests passed judgement on criminals. The ceiling of the pavilion, shown here, is decorated with minutely detailed depictions of the gruesome punishments awaiting sinners in hell and the heavenly rewards of the blameless.

The Mother Temple

Rising in a forest of pagoda-roofed *meru*, 900 feet (275 meters) up on the slopes of Gunung Agung, Pura Besakih is the mightiest of all Bali's myriad temples. This is the so-called "mother temple", once the royal place of worship for the old Gelgel kingdom and now a center of pilgrimage for Balinese of every caste and community. Hindu worship has gone on here since at least the thirteenth century, though there are older platforms beneath the temple foundations, probably once the shrines of a local belief system long before the first waves of Indian cultural influence washed ashore in Bali. Besakih is reached via a turning off the road that runs northwards from Klung-kung to Kintamani.

RIGHT There are 22 individual temples within the mighty Besakih complex, many featuring spectacular *meru* roofs. These tapering, pagoda-like towers are a classic feature of Balinese temple architecture. They are made from wood and thatched with black fiber from the *areng* palm. The towers are meant to represent Mount Meru, the mythical sacred peak of Hinduism, and they rise over a shrine dedicated to an individual god or deified ancestor. The number of roof tiers depends on the status of the god in question, though it is always an odd number, between three and eleven.

ABOVE Padangbai, seen from above. This pretty village in eastern Bali occupies a crescent-shaped bay sheltered by craggy headlands. It's the main ferry port for interisland traffic to Lombok, but beyond the harbor it's a sleepy place, with fine beaches nearby.
LEFT The coast around Candidasa in eastern Bali has developed a reputation as prime paragliding territory thanks to the way the inland mountains drop steeply down towards the coast here, generating excellent thermals, especially during the dry season when onshore breezes blow. The favored take-off site is a terraced clifftop at the eastern end of the Candidasa strip, from where experienced flyers can explore the coast in both directions. In Bali local sensibilities always need to be respected and it's important to avoid flying directly over temples.

The sleepy little harbor village of Padangbai on its horseshoe bay is the jumping-off point for journeys to Lombok, Nusa Penida and the Gili Islands, but it's also one of the most charming of Bali's accommodation centers, a lazy, low-key place where time slows to a snail's pace.

Further on the coast road traverses the easy-going resort of Candidasa, hard under the hills that slant steeply down to the shoreline here, while further east, beyond the regency town of Amlapura, an irresistible road rises into the green cleft between Gunung Agung and the outlying Lempuyung mountain, a spectacular setting for the water palace at Tirtagangga with its cool pools and slow-swimming carp. Beyond this the road drops to a harder, drier coastline and the string of villages known collectively as Amed, these days a favorite for divers, snorkelers and budget travelers.

Sideman: The Lost World

When the German artist Walter Spies, founding father of Bali's expat scene in the 1920s and 1930s, felt the need to escape the endless party of his own making in Ubud, he turned eastwards to a hidden bolt-hole in an isolated valley stretching inland from Klungkung towards the looming peak of Gunung Agung. It was a place where he could focus on his art, crafting dense, dark vistas of field and forest viewed from on high. At a glance his paintings seem fantastically stylized, but a first-hand view of the landscapes around Sideman reveals that they were not so far from reality.

Today Sideman still feels like a forgotten kingdom, locked in by high ridges. At night the lights of lonely villages float in inky blackness and the song of the frogs and insects in the rice fields creates a wall of noisy silence. In recent years those looking to escape the bustle of Ubud have taken to belatedly following Walter Spies' lead and a clutch of villas and guest houses have sprouted amongst the fields. But this remains one of the most beautiful and unspoiled corners of Bali, with the slow cycle of the seasons still setting the tone.

ABOVE Like most of eastern Bali, Sideman is dominated by the huge peak of Gunung Agung. The valley is a powerhouse of traditional agriculture, with terraced gardens of rice interspersed with beans, chili and myriad other crops.

ABOVE Amed's sheltered shorelines are framed by steep, scrubby hillsides and backed by a magnificent view of Gunung Agung. The waters offshore, meanwhile, are calm and clear, making this one of the best destinations for straight-off-the-beach snorkeling.
LEFT One of Bali's most celebrated dive sites is the wreck of the *Liberty*, a US Army transport ship, torpedoed by a Japanese submarine during World War II. Today it lies in the shallows off Tulamben.
RIGHT The "water palace" at Tirtagangga is one of the most sublime spots in Eastern Bali. Built by a Karangasem raja in the early twentieth century, the complex of pools, gardens and statuary is surrounded by rice fields.

NORTHERN BALI: THE MOUNTAIN CORE AND THE PLACID NORTH COAST

Even when they are thickly swaddled in monsoon thunderheads or modestly veiled behind dry season haze, the mountains that form the core of Bali are a powerful presence. The angle of the landscapes, tilted ever upwards, the fierce force of the streams plunging down in the opposite direction, and the way turbulent cloudscapes seems to find themselves trapped in the belly of the island all speak of great giants somewhere close at hand.

A trinity of mighty mountains stands towards the north of Bali. The largest, Gunung Agung, is a smooth cone, daggering into the cool airstreams at its 9,944-foot (3,030-meter) summit. But arcing west of here there are broken mountains, vast volcanic calderas blotched with lakes, ringed with ridges and haunted by mists. From Klungkung, Gianyar and Ubud roads strike upwards, the villages thinning and the palms giving way to pines before a huge hollow opens ahead the Batur crater below Kintamani, with its slug of clear blue water and heart of craggy volcanic rubble.

Further west another road from Denpasar passes through Mengwi and onwards, with a detour to the left leading to the epic amphitheater of rice terraces below Jatiluwuh, to another massif, that of Bratan. Up here there are strawberry fields and apple orchards, wildly exotic fruits in the Indonesian tropics, botanic gardens and half-timbered guest houses as well as the much-photographed Puru Ulun Danu Bratan temple, which seems to float like a feather on the surface of the Bratan crater lake. To the west, meanwhile, the village of Munduk levitates above the tangle of ridges that bend and buckle on their descent to the north coast.

This northern shoreline, hard beneath the mountain walls, is a world apart from the busy south and even the main settlement of Singaraja has the feel of a backwater for all its 80,000 inhabitants. There's a low-key resort development stretched along the black sand beaches at Lovina, west of Singaraja. But as you continue westwards through the palm groves and past the coves where bone-white outriggers are moored above the tideline, you are traveling into the region of Bali least troubled by tourism.

TOP Pura Ulun Danu Bratan, at the heart of Bali's central highlands near Bedugul, is one of the most photographed of all temples, and with good reason given its stunning lakeside location.
ABOVE MIDDLE Though Bali is overwhelmingly Hindu, the north of the island is home to small Buddhist communities. The Brahmavihara Arama temple is a major center of Buddhism, in the hills a short way west of Lovina.

ABOVE Lovina has become the dolphin-watching capital of Bali thanks to obliging pods of bottlenose dolphins which make their territory in the calm waters offshore. Visitors taking boat trips here are almost guaranteed a sighting.
OPPOSITE TOP Gunung Agung is not the only major mountain in Bali. A short way to the west is the Gunung Batur caldera, seen here, with its crater lake and accessible central peak.

Bali's Time-Honored Irrigation System

The classic vision of Bali is that of a steep-sided valley crafted into narrow steps, each shining like a fragment of glass at planting time or waist deep with golden grain as harvest approaches, a landscape like a work of art.

Bali is not alone in Indonesia as a land of remarkable rice farming. Many parts of Java, Lombok and Sulawesi also display formidable feats of terracing. But this most complex of field forms has a particular distinction in Bali thanks to its cultural significance. Every inch of irrigated Balinese farmland comes under the governance of a *subak*. There are well over a thousand of these traditional irrigation associations, each comprising every landowner within a particular network of ditches and canals.

Subak are governed by Bali's unique customary law and they are about more than just water. Each irrigation association doubles as a religious fraternity, with its own temple dedicated to the rice goddess Dewi Sri, one of the indigenous Indonesian deities co-opted into the unique pantheon of Balinese Hinduism. Some of the finest places to appreciate the complexities of *subak* operations are the terraced landscapes around Tegallalang and Jatiluwuh on the mountainsides north of Ubud.

RIGHT MIDDLE The rice terraces at Jatiluwih, on the south-facing slopes of the central mountains, are amongst the most spectacular in Bali. They cover a vast area and have been cited as a prime example of *subak* in operation.

ABOVE Although new technologies were introduced to Indonesian agriculture in the 1960s, rice farming in Bali, especially in the terraced hills, remains a labor-intensive operation. Planting of the rice seedlings in the flooded terraces is still done by hand.

THE WAVE-LASHED WEST

Bali's western regions feel like a land apart. The island stretches out here, almost as if to distance itself from the busy beach resorts of the south. Indeed, the tall mountains of East Java often seem closer at hand than Denpasar. The main road from the ferry terminal at Gilimanuk carries a ceaseless torrent of trucks and buses, an incongruous corridor of noise and grit amongst much wilder surrounds. The southwest facing coastline here is a lonely, wave-lashed place lined with wind-whipped palm trees, while to the north is the true wilderness of the West Bali National Park.

Heading into this region on a round-island journey from the direction of Lovina and Singaraja, you reach the little beach town of Pemuteran. The sheltered bay here is ringed with guest houses and resorts, but the whole place is so far removed from the other tourist centers that it has the castaway atmosphere of a forgotten community. There is excellent diving and snorkeling near here, not least around the offshore islet of Pulau Menjangan, perhaps the finest of all Bali's underwater destinations. Pemuteran is also a good base for journeys into the depths of the West Bali National Park, a world of light and shade drenched in a cascade of birdsong.

Heading back southwards towards Denpasar there's every reason to strike out from the main highway. There are important Hindu-Bali temples here, many of them well off the tour bus circuit, and there are also slowly growing coastal hideaways, the guarded secrets of a handful of itinerant surfers until a few years ago, now beginning to find space for those looking to maroon themselves in a little more comfort. Medewi and Balian are the foremost of these places. The final staging post of the west before the fleshpots of the south swing open their doors with the promise of bright lights is the coastal temple of Tanah Lot, braced against the freight train groundswell on a knuckle of black rock. It's a place that seethes with sightseers and crawls with souvenir hawkers of an afternoon, but arrive before midday and you'll find space to take in the view undisturbed.

TOP LEFT Though it's the Bukit Peninsula that gets most of the star attention and the beginners' waves of Kuta that attract the major crowds, there's excellent surf all along the exposed western coast from Canggu northwards to Medewi and beyond.
RIGHT The Bali starling, pictured here, is critically endangered. Also known as Rothschild's mynah, this striking white bird was once found all over the island until hunting for the caged bird trade pushed it to the brink of extinction. However, a successful captive breeding and release program has recently established a thriving population on offshore Nusa Penida, and another population survives in the forests of the West Bali National Park.

ABOVE Pura Tanah Lot, built on a rocky islet and facing the full brunt of the Indian Ocean surf, is one of the most dramatically situated temples in Bali. It is one of the *Sad Kahyangan*, the six holiest shrines of Balinese Hinduism. It is also one of the seven major sea temples. The name Tanah Lot means "Land-Sea", an obvious reference to the temple's setting. Like many of the most important religious sites in Bali, Tanah Lot is associated with Dang Hyang Nirartha, a semi-mythical Hindu priest and temple builder who traveled to Bali from Java in the mid-sixteenth century. He is credited with creating the essential architectural patterns of the island's temples.

RIGHT Pemuteran, pictured here, is tucked away at the northwest corner of Bali, far removed from busy resorts or hectic towns. It's still, at heart, a traditional fishing village but it is also home to a clutch of low-key resorts and guest houses. Most travelers come here to dive or snorkel. The waters offshore are clear and calm and hide some of Bali's best and most accessible dive sites. Further west lies Pulau Menjangan, "Deer Island". Accessible by boat and often visited from Pemuteran, it is part of the West Bali National Park and has superb coral gardens just offshore. The island is also home to a population of sambar, the large deer for which it is named.

A STRING OF SMALL WORLDS

In Nusa Tenggara, the "Islands of the Southeast", the idea of Indonesia as the world's greatest archipelago comes to the fore. The islands here, stretching eastwards from Bali to Timor, are a string of small worlds, each in view of its neighbors and yet each with its own utterly distinctive character.

History and culture take on an earthier tone hereabouts. Gone are the hulking classical temples of Java and the stately ceremonies of Bali. This is, instead, a place of thatched clan houses and ancestral tombs. And while the official religious affiliations of the region are a patchwork of Islam, Protestantism and Catholicism, Nusa Tenggara is a place where the older currents of *adat*, indigenous "custom", run deep.

When it came to travel, Nusa Tenggara was long the territory of hardy island-hoppers and surfing frontiersmen, happy to brave rickety ferries and bone-shattering bus rides. Much of the region is still deliciously distant from the beaten track, but thanks to improved air links it is now much more accessible.

LEFT Labuanbajo, at the western tip of Flores, is the gateway to the Komodo National Park. With its pretty harbor and maritime links to other islands, it's also a place redolent of the romance of travel in eastern Indonesia.

ABOVE In Nusa Tenggara the going gets slow. Winding mountain roads, like this one in Flores, make for long journey times, and public transport can be packed with passengers and cargo. Sometimes the roof is the most spacious place to ride!

LOMBOK: UNDER THE VOLCANO

Lombok has long labored in the shadow of its illustrious western neighbor, Bali. But while it has similar rice field and mountain vistas, it is every inch its own island. Its indigenous people are the Muslim Sasaks, and while it recognizably belongs to the broader cultural sphere of western Indonesia you can also sense the influence of the wilder lands beyond the Alas Strait to the east.

Lombok's capital is the city of Mataram. This was once the seat of the island's overlords, an offshoot of the Balinese royal house of Karangasem. Their influence is still there to see in the red-brick temples of the local Hindu population. The main base for visitors hereabouts is the endearingly sleepy beach town of Senggigi, but for those seeking to wriggle beneath the skin of Lombok the best bet is to travel beyond the last hotels along the road that skirts the northern coast.

The dominant presence here, as everywhere on Lombok, is the mighty Gunung Rinjani, an active volcano (geological instability is a fact of life here, as starkly illustrated by a major earthquake which shook Lombok in 2018, killing several hundred people and causing extensive damage). Rinjani is a cultural linchpin, and in the villages around Bayan on its northern flanks locals have maintained a syncretic belief system known as *Wetu Telu* alongside their more conventional Muslim observances.

There are enduring syncretic traditions on the southern flanks of the mountain too, especially around the pretty village of Tetebatu, but beyond here, south of the main cross-island highway, the landscape and atmosphere are very different—dry and empty save for the isolated modern airport. Eventually the hills descend to the little beach town of Kuta, a far cry from its Balinese namesake, standing on a crescent of pale sand with craggy coast stretching east and west.

TOP LEFT The Sasak people of Lombok have their own traditional martial art. Known as *Peresean*, it features fierce battles between competitors armed with a stick called a *penjalin*. Traditionally this was viciously edged with sharp grit or even broken glass, making the other piece of kit, a buffalo hide shield, particularly essential.
MIDDLE LEFT Lombok is an overwhelmingly rural island beyond the busy urban center of Mataram. Agriculture and fishing are still the major industries here and the island's traditional markets are full of local produce, from fresh vegetables to dried fish and peanuts. The name Lombok actually means "chili" and chili certainly features amongst the produce available.
LEFT There is very little development around the coasts of Lombok other than in the sleepy resort town of Senggigi and around Kuta on the southern littoral. There are a handful of hideaway resorts and castaway-style guest houses scattered further afield, but there are miles and miles of empty shorelines to be explored.

CLOCKWISE FROM TOP Gunung Rinjani is one of Indonesia's most magnificent mountains. More a massif than a single peak, it rises to 12,224 feet (3,726 meters) in the north of Lombok and can be seen from all corners of the island on a clear day. The vast caldera, a relic of a huge eruption thought to have taken place in the mid-thirteenth century, is filled with water. This lake is known as *Segara Anak*, "Child of the Sea", and it is considered sacred by local Hindus and in traditional Sasak belief. Hot springs, fueled by geothermal activity, spout at several points around the slopes. The volcano is very much still active, though the sporadic action is mostly confined to a small peak within the caldera known as *Gunung Baru*, "New Mountain", which can be seen beneath the highest point of the crater rim (**TOP**).

Getting to the top of the mountain, the second highest volcanic summit in Indonesia, topped only by Kerinci in Sumatra, involves a tough trek, but it's well worth the effort. The best route begins at the upland village of Sembalun Lawang, east of the mountain. From there an easy trail leads through grassy foothills before a steep climb brings hikers to a campsite on the crater rim, directly below the summit (**BOTTOM RIGHT**). The traditional approach is to set up camp here, then head upwards in the early hours of the morning, aiming to be at the summit in time for sunrise. It's a hard slog over steep scree slopes high enough for the draining effects of altitude to be apparent. But the rewards at the top more than compensate (**BOTTOM LEFT**).

On a clear day the view stretches from Gunung Agung on Bali to Gunung Tambora on Sumbawa, with a dramatic shadow effect created by the summit itself as the sun comes up over Sumbawa's serried black hills. Having made it back to camp, hikers usually follow an anticlockwise route around the caldera, with a second overnight stop followed by a descent through dense forest to the pleasant mountain village of Senaru.

The Gili Islands

Since the first hippies headed east in the 1960s there have always been certain places that attain fabled status on the budget travelers' grapevine. From generation to generation the location of these halcyon outposts of low-cost hedonism shifts, from Kathmandu to Ko Pha Ngan and from Goa to Vang Vieng. But for the last few decades a trio of tiny islets off the northwest corner of Lombok have clung firmly to their place on the rosters of backpackers' world wonders. The three Gili islands, Trawangan, Meno and Air, were once home to only a few hardy coconut farmers. Today they are visited by thousands of travelers, most now arriving by direct speedboat transfer from Bali. Though some old-timers bemoan overdevelopment, the islands are still beautiful, ringed with blinding white sand, and away from Gili Trawangan's party scene they are still seriously tranquil. The days of the penurious itinerants, frittering away dollar-a-day seasons in heaven, are largely a thing of the past, though. These days more travelers arrive pulling wheeled suitcases than lugging faded backpacks. The Gilis were shaken by the major earthquake that rocked Lombok in 2018, but escaped the worst damage and remain a paradisiacal place.

TOP Seen from above the low-lying geography of the Gilis is revealed, with Gili Air in the foreground, Meno in the middle distance and Trawangan furthest off.
TOP (INSET) The Gilis are a snorkelers' paradise, with extremely clear waters and good coral right off the beaches. There are excellent dive sites a little further off.
ABOVE RIGHT The Gilis were originally a backpackers' playground, with basic lodgings for world travelers on tight budgets. These days, however, they've gone decidedly upscale.

MIDDLE RIGHT Rush hour Gili Trawangan style. The secret of the islands' enduring charm in the face of tourist development is that they remain free from motorized land transport. The sandy lanes are plied only by rickety horse carts and bicycles.
BOTTOM RIGHT An absence of officialdom and the melting pot influence of international and domestic tourism have created an easy-going beach scene on Gili Trawangan, with plenty of laid-back socializing and more than a few local wannabe Bob Marleys.

LEFT Journeys east of Lombok can be undertaken the old-fashioned way by local buses and ferries. But these days many people choose instead to travel with a local cruise company, some using traditional *pinisi*-style boats.
BELOW The town of Sumbawa Besar, literally "Big Sumbawa", is a former royal capital, the erstwhile seat of a sultan who presided over the western half of the island in precolonial times. The old wooden place, known locally as *Istana Tua* or *Dalam Loka*, still stands in a quiet neighborhood. Dating from 1885, it was supposedly built without using a single metal nail.

SUMBAWA: AN ISLAND IN BETWEEN

Sumbawa is an island in between. This is as far as the influence of Java's ancient Hindu-Buddhist culture ever reached with any confidence and as far as Islam spread in the centuries that followed. It is also the easternmost island before Melanesian ethnicities begin to dominate. Sumbawa's head might point towards Bali and Java, but its twisting tail stretches towards Papua.

This is a wild and sparsely populated place, but for explorations away from the masses, Sumbawa has much to offer. In the far west, around the mining town of Maluk, there are surf beaches with sand as fine as caster sugar. The town of Sumbawa Besar, meanwhile, is the faded seat of a sultanate, still home to a rickety wooden palace and a busy morning market. Off the north coast, Pulau Moyo is a hunk of coral-fringed jungle, home to one of eastern Indonesia's most exclusive and isolated resorts.

The eastern half of the island—home to another former sultanate at Bima—is dominated by the hulk of Gunung Tambora, which in 1815 blew itself to pieces in the most destructive volcanic eruption in recorded history. The only real hub of tourist accommodation on the whole island is on the lonely southern shoreline at Hu'u, known to the surfers who travel here as Lakeys. It's a place where the sunsets blaze like a furnace over the empty Indian Ocean and where the rest of the world seems impossibly distant.

BELOW LEFT The *becak* is the Indonesian version of the ubiquitous Asian pedicab. Passengers sit up front and the driver rides behind. Once the major mode of suburban transport across the archipelago, they have vanished from many major cities (*becak* are forbidden in central Jakarta and unknown in Bali). However, brightly decorated examples still ply the streets of Sumbawa Besar.
BELOW Vendors and shoppers share a moment's gossip in the market at Poto Tano, entry point to Sumbawa for travelers coming from Lombok by ferry. As in Lombok, most people in Sumbawa are Muslim. In the east of the island, however, amongst the highland Dou Donggo people, traces of older religious beliefs still survive alongside universal Muslim practice.

Komodo: Here Be Dragons

In Nusa Tenggara the map can still be marked with the words "here be dragons", for the bony outcrops of land that rise from the seething seas between Sumbawa and Flores are truly home to reptilian monsters, seemingly raised from the land of legends. Known to the locals as *ora* and to the rest of the world as Komodo dragons, these giant monitor lizards, some growing over 10 feet (3 meters) in length, live only on Komodo itself, the neighboring island of Rinca, a couple of other little outcrops, and in isolated spots in western Flores. They usually prey on the unfortunate deer, buffalo and wild horses that share their territory.

The islands are a national park, with the undersea attractions for divers and snorkelers matching the megafauna on dry land. Until recently a visit here came only after a grueling island-hopping odyssey eastwards from Bali. But these days the park is one of Indonesia's major tourist destinations, usually accessed via the charming, if increasingly busy, town of Labuanbajo in Flores, with its good flight connections, hotels, dive shops and restaurants. Most people visit Komodo itself on day trips from Labuanbajo or from one of the little island resorts nearby.

BELOW The Komodo National Park is made up of 29 small islands, with the eponymous Komodo and neighboring Rinca the biggest of the lot. They are dry places, typified by tawny grasslands and low scrub.

TOP Though they are predatory, most visitors to the Komodo National Park only ever see the dragons in docile mood, moving sluggishly or lounging in the hot sun. They do, however, sometimes fight each other over food or territory.

ABOVE The Manggarai people of western Flores have a unique tradition known as *Caci*. Part dance, part fight and steeped in complex symbolism, it involves two men engaged in a ritual battle with rattan whips and buffalo hide shields.

FLORES: THE ISLAND OF FLOWERS

A rattletrap bus grinds through a hairpin bend on a mountain road. Wooden crosses, a little crooked, rise dark against the sky on the summit of a dragon's-back ridge. And a lone outrigger creeps towards a blue horizon beneath an upended triangle of sail. Flores has a curious magic all of its own.

This mountainous, overwhelmingly green island takes its name from the Portuguese word for "flowers". The influence of the long-departed Iberian colonialists is still plain to see in the dominant Catholic religion, which in places finds itself part of a curious amalgam along with ancestor-venerating *adat*. The tourist upsurge around the Komodo National Park has turned the once sleepy harbor village of Labuanbajo at the westernmost tip of the island into a boom town. But those heading east into the hills along the twists and turns of the Trans-Flores Highway quickly find an older world reasserting.

High in the central mountains the town of Bajawa rests in a bowl of green ground. This is the heartland of the Ngada people, who have cleaved closely to their traditional way of life. The villages hereabouts still have shrines for the ancestral spirits. Beyond Bajawa the highway descends to the coast and the sweltering port of Ende, once a haunt of slave-trading pirates, then wriggles its way back into the hills, passing the misty mountain of Kelimutu where a trio of crater lakes are vividly colored by volcanic minerals. Further on, on the north coast, the scrappy town of Maumere is the gateway to isolated dive resorts.

Beyond here there's an unavoidable sense of road's end approaching and it arrives in the little town of Larantuka, with its grazing goats and its stations of the cross. But journeys do not have to finish here. Out across the water Nusa Tenggara continues in a smattering of still smaller, wilder, stranger landfalls and at the dockside a white boat is waiting....

TOP Flores has many traditional village communities, such as the striking Wae Rebo in the Manggarai district. The houses here are known as *mbaru niang* and each contains five levels beneath a thick cladding of thatch.
ABOVE MIDDLE A fisherman from Maumere heads to shore with a simple outrigger canoe.
ABOVE Kelimutu's remarkable multicolored crater lakes seen from on high. The lakes periodically change color as the mineral composition of the volcanic vents below alters.

Sabu: On the Edge of the Map

Some islands seem to belong to another century and the tiny outcrop of Sabu, halfway between Timor and Sumba, is such a place. It dangles in the abyss of the Indian Ocean at the end of the thinnest and most frayed of connecting threads, a fifteen-hour ferry ride from Kupang a couple of times a week or a frequently cancelled flight aboard a tiny twin-prop plane. When you first catch sight of its shores, an endless rank of lontar palms backing a thin line of sand and surf, you know that little has changed since the great maritime explorer Captain James Cook dropped anchor here two and a half centuries ago.

Only a handful of outsiders make it to Sabu each year, mostly intrepid surfers or Protestant missionaries, and accommodation and dining options in the tiny capital, Seba, are basic to say the least. But any traveler who does step down from the ferry will be welcomed like a long-lost friend. There are perfect beaches just outside town, lingering traces of the indigenous *Jingi Tiu* religion in the lontar-thatched villages of the interior and a powerful sense of having somehow reached an island lying outside the normal bounds of time and space.

ABOVE Gathering mildly alcoholic fermented sap from lontar palms requires a head for heights.
ABOVE RIGHT Stone altars, known as *nada ae*, at the traditional Sabu village of Namata.

ABOVE The town of Larantuka at the easternmost tip of Flores maintains a unique Catholic heritage. The faith was introduced in the sixteenth century by the Portuguese, but after the Protestant Dutch achieved supremacy the Larantuka community was largely cut off from coreligionists for hundreds of years, allowing distinct local traditions to emerge. The annual Easter parade, shown here, focussing on an ancient statue of the Virgin Mary and a mysterious relic of Christ, is a huge event.

OPPOSITE TOP Seen from the waterfront in Lewoleba on neighboring Lembata, Adonara's Ile Boleng volcano rises into a sunset sky. This currently dormant peak dominates the island and has a strong role in local traditions. As on many other peaks in Nusa Tenggara, annual offerings of live chickens amongst other things are made at the crater. It is also forbidden to discuss topics relating to the sea or boats while on the mountain slopes.

ABOVE MIDDLE Hunters from Lamalera on the lookout for a whale. This isolated coastal community is, along with Lamakera across the strait on Solor, one of the last traditional whaling villages.

ABOVE A family poses in Takpala, one of the many traditional villages on Alor. This community of wood-and-thatch houses perches on a high hillside and is a stronghold of the Abui, one of Alor's many cultural groups.

POINTS EAST: FROM ADONARA TO ALOR

There are ghosts out amongst the islands that trail from the easternmost end of Flores: ghosts of a vanished Portuguese empire, ghosts of influences from other shores and, if you believe the stories, real ghosts haunting the forest fringes. Though Alor, the largest and easternmost of the islands, has air links with Kupang and a smattering of dive resorts, for the most part this is a region outside even the most ambitious of island-hopping itineraries. But for those happy to voyage beyond the writ of guidebooks and to accept rough rides and basic accommodation, this is one of the most intoxicatingly strange corners of Indonesia to explore.

The westernmost part of the chain comes in the form of two small islands. Solor is a slender ridge of land, the seat of Portuguese traders in the sixteenth century, while neighboring Adonara is dominated by the cone-shaped peak of Ile Boleng. There is some very basic accommodation in the harbor township of Waiwerang, and in the deep hills there are villages where ancestors are appeased with offerings of palm wine.

The rugged bulk of Lembata rises further to the east. Overland travel beyond the little capital of Lewoleba is tough, but on the craggy southern coast there's one community that's long been a favorite of anthropologists and documentary makers, the village of Lamalera, home to some of the last traditional whale hunters on earth, men who take on their giant prey with hand-thrown spears and open boats. For those who tackle the journey, there are basic homestays and very warm welcomes to be had in Lamalera.

Further east, the island of Pantar is pierced by the jagged volcanic peak of Sirung, then across a deep strait a long inlet leads to Kalabahi, capital of Alor. The diving here is amongst the best in Indonesia and there is decent accommodation for underwater adventurers. But there is much to see inland too, in deeply traditional villagers where locals tell unsettling tales of the dragon spirits that guard the island.

TIMOR & ROTE: INDONESIA'S OUTER LIMITS

The air smells different in West Timor. It is dry, faintly scented with charcoal and honey, more like that of the Australian outback than of the Indonesian tropics. And little wonder. Darwin is just beyond the southern horizon while Jakarta is worlds away. The little city of Kupang has the only major airport hereabouts, so it's a natural gateway for East Nusa Tenggara. But slow the pace before racing onwards. West Timor and its little neighbor Rote have their own attractions here at the very limits of Indonesia's vastness.

In 1789 Captain Bligh stumbled ashore in Kupang at the end of a 3,816-mile (6,140-km) journey from the South Pacific in an open boat after the mutiny aboard HMS *Bounty*. The town has grown in the centuries since but it still feels like an outpost at the ends of the earth, a place where motley castaways still wash up on the seafront. However, the real magic of Timor lies inland, especially in the hills around Soe where traditions of *ikat* weaving are strong. In the stand-alone settlement of Boti, the influences of Christianity, colonialism and Indonesian bureaucracy have all been kept at bay.

To the south, meanwhile, the island of Rote rises, a slender fragment of limestone speckled with lontar palms. Nembrala, on the southernmost shore, is the easternmost outpost of the Indonesian surf circuit, a perfect coral beach fronting a long slab of offshore reef, beyond which there is nothing until Australia.

ABOVE The traditional house of West Timor is the *lopo*, a conical structure with a thatched roof reaching right down to ground level, with access provided only by a single low doorway. These days many families build a more conventional house to live in, whether of concrete and tin or wood and thatch. But they often also maintain an adjoining *lopo*, as in this image, as a kitchen and storage room.

TOP RIGHT West Timor is one of the strongholds of *ikat* weaving in Nusa Tenggara and markets are great places to find pieces, sold mainly to locals rather than as souvenirs. Here a man visiting the market in Soe sports an *ikat* scarf with the orange color scheme popular hereabouts.

RIGHT MIDDLE AND BELOW In the market at Soe in West Timor fighting cocks and *sirih-pinang* are amongst the wares on offer. *Sirih-pinang*, usually called areca or betel nut in English, is a mildly narcotic concoction. It is chewed throughout Indonesia but is particularly popular in Nusa Tenggara. *Pinang*, the round green areca, which can be spotted laid out for sale in these images, is the active part of the package. It can produce a slight light-headedness. It is chewed along with *sirih*, a kind of catkin, a dab of lime paste and sometimes gambier leaf, cloves and tobacco. The action of the lime and nut produces livid red saliva, hence the luridly stained smiles of many Nusa Tenggara locals.

LEFT The *Pasola* is a spectacle like no other in eastern Indonesia. This ritual battle on horseback is at the heart of traditional cultural life in coastal regions of West Sumba. The *Pasola* is held at four different locations between February and March, with the exact dates determined by the appearance of *nyale*, a kind of sea worm which wash up in the shallows on certain nights during the rainy season. Once the *nyale* have appeared, battle can commence, with dozens of riders hurling wooden spears at one another. Not so long ago these spears were tipped with metal, and while they are now blunted injuries are still common, and indeed expected.

SUMBA: IKAT AND ANCESTORS

Sumba seems to have been squeezed out by the other islands of Nusa Tenggara. It lies to the south of the main chain, a slug of stony ground that seems almost to be tumbling away into the depths of the southern Indian Ocean. Its limestone geography underscores its difference. There are no volcanoes here and no dominant mountains, only a mass of ridges and escarpments angling towards lost shorelines. Sumba stands apart culturally too, for this is one of the last true bastions of indigenous religious traditions in Indonesia. Though church bells toll island-wide of a Sunday and virtually everyone is officially Protestant, the older belief system, known as *Marapu*, which simply means "Ancestors", is still paid much more than mere lip service out in the numberless villages that rise in conspiratorial huddles from the hilltops. Sumba is also one of the greatest strongholds of cloth weaving and its strikingly patterned blankets are prized by serious *ikat* aficionados.

Waingapu is the main town in the east of the island. There are many villages with a strong weaving tradition in easy striking distance of town, while a journey north along the coast leads into one of the most unexpected landscapes in all Indonesia: vast empty acreages of tawny grassland stalked by herds of hardy horses. On the highest ridge here is the village of Wunga, a community that stands out even in Sumba for its dogged adherence to tradition: the houses here are built without nails.

In the west of the island the little town of Waikabubak is the best base for explorations of the traditional heartlands. Some of the most accessible traditional villages, most notably Tarung, actually rise from hilltops within the town, while there are dozens of other such places in the hills to the south.

West Sumba is famed for its *Pasola* festival, a rousing ritual battle fought on horseback between rival villages in the late months of the wet season each year. Surfers, meanwhile, set their sights on the remote reefs of the southern coast, especially those around the ultra-exclusive and ultra-isolated resort at Nihiwatu.

ABOVE MIDDLE Beyond the few small towns most people in Sumba still live in hamlets dominated by houses with remarkable tower roofs, some now made of tin but many still thatched as here at Praijing, a short distance from Waikabubak. Known locally as *uma*, the design of these houses features a delicate ritual balance between male and female elements.

ABOVE Sumba is one of the great frontiers of surf travel in Indonesia. The southern coast is dotted with high-class breaks which see only a fraction of the crowds that mob Bali and far fewer traveling surfers than even nearby Sumbawa. Many visit on charter boats out of Kupang but those who go it alone get to experience the onshore attractions too.

THE ISLAND OF GOLD

When the scribes of ancient India wrote of the mysterious territory that lay on the eastern side of the Bay of Bengal they called it Swarnadwipa, "the island of gold". Today Sumatra is still an enigma, a land of deep forests, unexplored uplands, swampy deltas and wild shores.

Sumatra is vast, as big as Spain, and yet it is astonishingly empty, home to just 50 million people. If you arrive from the crowded spaces of Bali and Java, Sumatra's wildness can overwhelm. Distances here are enormous, and though recent deforestation has left the jungles of the eastern lowlands a little threadbare there is still an abundance of untrammeled emptiness.

Sumatra's history is suitably shadowy. In the first millennium CE mighty maritime empires rose from the eastern swamps, as indeed did the prototype of the Malay language which would soon become the lingua franca of the entire region. But today these kingdoms are little more than names in inky textbooks and a few crumbling mounds of red brick deep in the forest.

Most travelers coming to Sumatra stick to a small and richly rewarding circuit of stellar sights in striking distance of the gritty northern city of Medan. But those who step a little further afield will find much more to explore out there in Sumatra's great green vastness.

LEFT Three Minangkabau women showing off their lavish traditional outfits at a festival. The Minangkabau, whose homeland is in the hills of West Sumatra, are one of the major cultural groups of Sumatra.

OPPOSITE BOTTOM Banda Aceh's grand Baiturrahman Mosque is quite unlike most Indonesian Islamic architecture, with its Mughal-style domes and arches and bone-white masonry. It was actually designed by an Italian architect and built in 1879 to replace an earlier, more typically Indonesian mosque destroyed during the long conflict between Acehnese rulers and Dutch colonial forces.

RIGHT Last light in Mentawai. This chain of offshore islands is one of the most deeply traditional areas in all of Indonesia. Long isolated by stormy seas and challenging terrain, the major historical events on the Sumatran mainland had little impact here.

BELOW Lake Toba, at the heart of northern Sumatra, is a prized destination for travelers and a stronghold of the local Batak culture. The lake has its origins in one of the greatest volcanic eruptions ever known. Around 75,000 years ago an eruption a hundred times more powerful even than that of Tambora in 1815 created the vast caldera now filled by the lake.

ABOVE The Maimun Palace of Medan, once the seat of the Deli sultanate, was designed in the 1880s by a Dutch architect. It features a fusion of Italian and Islamic elements, decorated in the yellow color scheme of the royal house. **LEFT** A local man at rest in Medan's Grand Mosque. The mosque, which can be visited by non-Muslims outside of prayer times, displays a strong Turkish influence blended with odd Latinate touches in its interior. **BELOW** Medan's Grand Mosque, the *Mesjid Raya*, was built in the early 1900s at the request of Sultan Makmun Al-Rasyid. Like several other grand buildings of the period, it was designed by a European architect in a fusion style. **OPPOSITE BELOW** Set in the Karo Highlands, Berastagi was once a cool retreat for overheated plantation managers and colonial officials. Today it's a favored weekend getaway for Medan residents while the looming Gunung Sinabung volcano attracts hardy hikers.

NORTHERN SUMATRA: LAKES, MOUNTAINS AND ORANGUTANS

The city of Medan, close to the eastern seaboard of North Sumatra province, is a heaving Asian metropolis, an anomaly in this under-populated island. It has a few flashes of fascination amidst the mayhem: the elegant Mesjid Raya, the city's main mosque, the nearby palace of the Deli sultanate, and the various traces of the city's heyday as the hub of a colonial plantation economy. Most visitors, however, head for the hills as quickly as possible.

Four hours northwest of Medan the jungle village of Bukit Lawang, on the edge of the deep wilderness of the Gunung Leuser National Park, has a gently intoxicating community vibe and the world's most personable community of wild orangutans lumbering long-limbed through the surrounding forests. Also in easy striking distance of the city, the tiny village of Tangkahan gets far fewer visitors but is the place to go for elephant-back explorations of the surrounding forests.

TOP RIGHT Sumatra is one of the two regions on earth where orangutans are found in the wild; the other is Borneo. Bukit Lawang, northwest of Medan, is one of the best places on earth for close-up encounters with these great apes. Rehabilitated captive orangutans have been returned to the wild here.

RIGHT Tucked away in the forested countryside north of Bukit Lawang is the little community of Tangkahan, a center for low-key eco-tourism, where elephants are used to patrol against loggers and poachers and to carry tourists into the jungle. Visitors can also help give these huge animals their daily bath.

LEFT The countryside around Lake Toba is dotted with Toba Batak villages. These communities feature dramatic traditional architecture in the form of houses with extravagantly accentuated roof gables and decorative woodwork. The houses here are not as overwhelmingly huge as those in the neighboring Karo Batak regions but the roof ridge is more flamboyantly curved and there is a communal balcony at the front. Traditionally four families would occupy each house though these days they are usually given over to a single household.

BELOW Passengers aboard a local ferry at Tuk Tuk, Lake Toba. The center of the lake is taken up by a large island, Samosir. With a ruggedly beautiful interior and a tranquil shoreline, it's little wonder that this place has long had a special position on the Southeast Asia travel circuit. Samosir is actually connected to the mainland by a bridge in the northwest but the nicest way to arrive is by boat to the Tuk Tuk peninsula in the east.

Swinging southwards into the Karo Highlands, the hill town of Berastagi was once the place where overheated Dutch planters sought to escape the sweltering heat of the lowlands. Today it serves the same purpose for weekending Medan residents. The town is the portal to the homeland of the Karo Batak, and in outlying villages like Lingga their tall, horn-roofed traditional dwellings have been preserved. Berastagi is also prime hiking territory while the nearby peaks of Sibayak and Sinabung are prime day trips.

The true centerpiece of North Sumatra lies a little further south. Shining like a polished piece of lapis lazuli in the green baize of the Sumatran highlands, Danau Toba is Southeast Asia's largest lake, filling the collapsed caldera of a vast prehistoric volcano. At its center is Samosir, an almost-island, barely connected to the mainland by a slender isthmus. Samosir has been charming travelers for decades with the easy-going warmth of the local Christian Batak community and the endlessly appealing vision of distant ridges rising over the lake.

RIGHT MIDDLE A church in the countryside near Lake Toba. In the 1860s, after desultory efforts by British, Dutch and French missionaries earlier in the century, the German Rhenish Mission began to work in the Toba area. Protestant Christianity caught on amongst the Toba Bataks and to a lesser extent in other Batak regions, and by the early twentieth century it was a key part of Toba Batak identity with the German mission superseded by an independent Batak-governed church authority. **RIGHT** Local Bataks put on a performance at the village of Simanindo at the northern tip of Samosir. A grand traditional house here, once the residence of a Batak king, is now an interesting museum. **OPPOSITE BOTTOM** A trio of traditional houses on Samosir look out across the tranquil Lake Toba towards the mainland. The lake is ringed by high ridges which are, in fact, a vast volcanic caldera.

Aceh: A New Travel Frontier

On the map Aceh seems to be straining northwestward as if seeking to escape from the rest of Indonesia. And, indeed, for well over a century that is exactly what this restive province has been trying to do. Resistance to Dutch rule here rolled over into similar resistance to Indonesian governance, resistance which only ended in the wake of the devastating 2004 tsunami. Though Aceh has a reputation as the most conservatively Islamic corner of Indonesia, culturally sensitive travelers are now discovering a welcoming new frontier for adventure, from pristine diving off Pulau Weh to jungle trekking in the cool and cloudy Gayo Highlands.

ABOVE One of the emerging treasures of Aceh is Laut Tawar Lake. The name means "Freshwater Sea". This huge body of water, deep in the mountains, is Aceh's answer to Lake Toba.

CENTRAL SUMATRA:
FROM SEA TO SHINING SEA

A ridge of beetling mountains runs the entire length of Sumatra. Cleaving close to the Indian Ocean seaboard, the western flanks of this range, known as the Bukit Barisan, slope steeply to the coast. In the opposite direction, meanwhile, they drop to a great slab of swampy lowlands, which fade eventually into the Straits of Melaka.

The mountains are at their most accessible in the middle of Sumatra, just below the point where the equator spans the island. These highlands are the homeland of the most far-famed of all Sumatra's ethnic groups, the Minagkabau. This matrilineal society has thrown up dozens of intellectuals, politicians and poets over the decades. It has also produced Indonesia's most beloved of regional cooking styles, the spicy, oily smorgasbord that is Padang cuisine.

Gateway to the Minangkabau region, and to the surfers' paradise of the Mentawai Islands, is the coastal city of Padang. Up the winding highway east of here is the mountain town of Bukittinggi, which is ringed by high peaks. The smoking cone of Marapi, near-namesake of the better known Javanese mountain Merapi, is the most accessible for trekkers. Deep amidst the locked ridges of the Bukit Barisan an hour and a half west of town is Danau Maninjau's lozenge of blue water. To the south, meanwhile, lie the seemingly limitless reaches of the Kerinci-Seblat National Park, one of the largest and least visited of all Indonesia's scheduled wild places, haunt of tigers and, according to local folklore, the *orang pendek*, a miniature Sumatran answer to the sasquatch.

The roads that run across the Bukit Barisan descend eastwards into the low-lying provinces of Riau and Jambi, where Sumatra swells to fill its generous portion of the globe. This is sweaty, steamy country, spiked with oil fields and palm oil plantations, laced with muddy rivers and finally fraying away amidst muddy coastal islets and inlets. Riau's maritime section stretches to the boom-time islands of Batam and Bintan, near neighbors of Singapore.

TOP On the edge of Bukittinggi lies the deep Sianok Canyon, a river-carved gorge thick with greenery. A large colony of fruit bats roosts here. **ABOVE MIDDLE** The Minangkabau regions of West Sumatra are home to some of the most impressive traditional architecture anywhere in Indonesia. Known as *rumah gadang*, literally "big house", they are built on a grand scale and traditionally occupied by multiple households, each headed, in accordance with matrilineal Minangkabau custom, by a woman. **ABOVE** Bull racing, with prize beasts pulling sled-like platforms across a freshly ploughed and flooded rice field, is a high-octane Minangkabau sport.

TOP Bukittinggi's central landmark is the *Jam Gadang*, the "Big Clock", seen here towering over the main square with the dark hulk of Gunung Singgalang in the background. **ABOVE MIDDLE** Tranquil Lake Maninjau, west of Bukittinggi, sees far fewer visitors than Lake Toba further north, but ringed by green ridges it is every bit as beautiful. **ABOVE** The glorious smorgasbord that is Padang cuisine can be sampled anywhere in Indonesia thanks to the long tradition of emigration from the Minangkabau regions. But the best place to try it, naturally enough, is in its place of provenance. Restaurants in Padang or Bukittinggi are good places to start.

The Mentawai Chain: A Necklace of Islands Off Sumatra's West Coast

Flanking the western coast of Sumatra, around 100 miles (160 km) offshore, is a long necklace of islands. Though they are dwarfed by the Sumatran mainland, some are as big as Bali. Others are the merest dabs of sand and coral, barely raising their heads above sea level. From Simeulue in the north through Nias, the Mentawai chain and all the way to lonely Enggano, this has long been a true frontier. Deeply traditional cultures have survived here long into the modern era. There had been little contact with the Indonesian authorities, still less with tourism.

The pioneers of travel here, besides the intrepid anthropologists who have always been fascinated by the megalithic culture of Nias, were surfers, and both Nias and Mentawai still rank amongst the most fabled of surfing destinations, with live-aboard charters still scouting out new breaks each season. These days, though, it is not only wave-riders and academics who travel to these islands. Nias, now largely recovered from the 2004 tsunami, is the easiest island to visit independently but Mentawai offers the wildest adventures. Even the main island in the chain, Siberut, is still thickly swaddled in primary rainforest, making it one of the finest places for jungle trekking in Indonesia.

Though traveling surfers (**TOP**) have helped open Mentawai to other tourists in recent decades, this offshore archipelago was long more isolated from the outside world than almost any other part of Indonesia. Neither Hindu-Buddhism, Islam nor Dutch colonialism had much impact here. Though today Christianity and the Indonesian state are firmly established, many locals still sport traditional tattoos (**ABOVE**) and maintain old customs.

Riau, Bangka and Belitung: The Eastern Islands

The Palembang sultanate, a turbulent kingdom which rose to glory on the banks of the Musi River in the sixteenth century, earned its riches from the export of tin, mined on two craggy granite islands which lay off the eastern coast of its mainland territory. Today these islands, Bangka and Belitung, are still colored by their mining heritage, not least in their large ethnic Chinese communities, descendants of laborers who came to dig for ore in centuries past. But they are no post-industrial wastelands. Instead, they are best known for their boulder-strewn beaches and clear waters. Belitung, in particular, has found status as an alternative to Bali for young travelers from Jakarta.

ABOVE The slender white tower of a Dutch-era lighthouse, built in 1882, rises over the islet of Lengkuas off the northwest coast of Belitung. **BELOW** Part of the Riau archipelago, Bintan, just a short ferry ride from Singapore or the neighboring industrialized island of Batam, is an easy getaway for city slickers. There are decent beaches here and some high-end resorts.

SUMATRA'S DEEP SOUTH: FAR FROM THE MADDING CROWD

The blunt southern tail of Sumatra angles down towards the Java Sea, a 150-mile (240-km) reach of lowlands to the east and the final flourish of the Bukit Barisan rising beyond 10,000 feet (3,050 meters) at its highest peaks to the west. This is a region of Sumatra that precious few travelers ever visit, yet there is much to see. Ramshackle stilt houses stand in shady forest groves, an open boat creeps along a wide white river, manicured tea gardens rumple up towards unseen summits and on the skeleton shoreline of the Indian Ocean the ghosts of empires past still linger on.

The slender slip of territory belonging to Bengkulu, hard on the western seaboard, is one of Indonesia's loneliest provinces, a narrow ledge of level land with the dark hills of the Bukit Barisan on one side and the driving surf of the Indian Ocean on the other. The eponymous capital city is a slow-moving place, still marked in quiet corners by the relics of the ill-fated British outpost that once occupied this coast. Amongst the better known British residents here was Thomas Stamford Raffles, famed as the co-founder of the British settlement at Singapore. In the hills above town the gruesome plant that bears his name, *Rafflesia arnoldi*, can still be found. This largest of flowers gives off a pungent odor of decay to attract insects.

Further into the hills and across the provincial border into South Sumatra province the little town of Pagaralam is the hub of the temperate Pasemah Highlands, with their weird carved megaliths, their misty tea gardens and their dominant mountain, the mighty volcanic monster that is Gunung Dempo, towering into the running cloud.

Further south along the chain of the Bukit Barisan and straddling the border between South Sumatra and the southern-most province of Lampung, there is a hidden lake, Danau Ranau, cupped between dark ridges and many miles from any major town, while still further south, at the ultimate terminus of the island, the Way Kambas National Park welcomes visitors for elephant encounters and the closest thing Indonesia has to a proper safari experience.

ABOVE The huge *Rafflesia arnoldi* flower is a parasite. It attaches itself to vines and draws liquid and nutrients from them. The largest examples can weigh as much as 22 pounds (10 kg).

Sumatra's Lost Kingdoms

Lost amongst the tangled deltas of Sumatra's southeastern lowlands, the cities of Jambi and Palembang today feel infinitely isolated from the heartlands of modern Indonesia. And yet this was the region where, in the first millennium CE, the model of maritime trading power that came to bind the archipelago into a loose whole in the coming centuries first emerged.

The names of the trading states that rose on the middle reaches of the rivers here are little more than ghostly echoes today, whispering from the works of Chinese chroniclers: Ko-ying, P'u-lei, Kantoli, Melayu and Srivijaya. There is virtually nothing to show from the mightiest of these polities, Srivijaya, which is believed to have been based at Palembang. But its successor, Melayu, has left enigmatic marks in the forest along the banks of the Batang Hari River outside Jambi. The crumbling red-brick

ruins of the Muaro Jambi temple complex, dating back to the eleventh and twelfth centuries, stretch for miles through the trees, but for hundreds of years they were forgotten by everyone but a handful of locals. Today a few structures have been sensitively restored but most remain in a state of atmospheric decrepitude and chances are you'll have the place to yourself.

TOP Despite its abundant rainfall and wealth of volcanoes, Sumatra does not have the supremely rich and readily worked soils of Java and Bali and so has never supported such large populations. Historically, rice was often imported from Java to make up the shortfall. There are pockets of rice growing, however, such as here in Bengkulu, with the dark ridge of the Bukit Barisan rising inland. **ABOVE MIDDLE** The Way Kambas National Park is an elephant stronghold. Domestic elephants are kept here for patrols and tours but there is also a herd of around 200 wild elephants at large in the forest. **ABOVE** The mighty Gunung Dempo looms over the Pasemah Highlands near Pagaralam. The area, with its temperate climate, was developed for growing tea in the late nineteenth century and tea gardens still cloak the lower slopes.

ABOVE The temples of Mauro Jambi might not be as spectacular as the grand edifices of Java, but with their remote and little visited jungle location they are hard to beat when it comes to atmosphere. Constructed between the seventh and twelfth centuries, the lack of readily available stone in these lowlands meant that builders used red brick instead.

INTO THE HEART OF BORNEO

Borneo. The word is like a great pool of darkness in the world's imagination, roiling with half-remembered visions of hornbills and headhunters. The southern two-thirds of this, the planet's third largest island, are occupied by the Indonesian provinces known collectively as Kalimantan, a land of long river journeys, orangutan encounters and sojourns in river towns where ghosts from the novels of Joseph Conrad still linger.

For hundreds of years a thin patina of outside influence has clung to the coast of Kalimantan. Far back in the first millennium CE there were shady Hindu-Buddhist states here, which later gave way to Muslim-ruled estuary sultanates, home to Malays, Chinese and Arabs, drawn to trade in the outlandish goods that came down in longboats from the hinterland: gold, diamonds, camphor and rhino horn. The unmapped interior, meanwhile, was the preserve of the dozens of Dayak tribes dwelling in smoky longhouses or wandering footloose through the forest and, as anyone on the coast would tell you, displaying a definite habit of headhunting.

Today the headhunters have made way for loggers and oilmen, but Kalimantan still has a curious magic and an enduring sense that, if you just keep traveling far enough upriver, you might find yourself in another century.

LEFT The Meratus Mountains extend a slender arm of high ground along the eastern edge of the great floodplains of the Barito and Kapuas rivers, reaching almost to the sea close to Banjarmasin. The rugged mountain terrain here has saved the region from the ravages of logging and plantation agriculture and allowed the Meratus Dayaks to maintain a strong cultural identity. There's a low-key tourist industry here based around the village of Loksado, with fine views of the mountains from the nearby Bukit Langara viewpoint, shown here, and excellent trekking opportunities.

RIGHT The remarkably humanlike proboscis monkey is one of the most intriguing of all Kalimantan's forest-dwelling creatures. They are found across the island of Borneo but they prefer low-lying areas, especially on the fringes of lakes, rivers and estuaries. They live in small family groups, such as that shown here, headed by a single male, identifiable by a more pronounced nose. A colloquial Indonesian name for the species is *monyet Belanda*, "Dutch monkey". As far as locals are concerned, the pot-bellied, long-nosed simians look a lot like colonial-era Dutchmen!

RIGHT An old boat, gradually rotting away on the sandy shore of tiny Pulau Sangalaki, an island in the sprawling Derawan Archipelago, which lies off the eastern coast of Kalimantan. The largest of the islands in the group is Maratua, a remarkable sickle of land rising along the northern rim of a vast coral atoll. There's excellent diving to be had here. The islands are sparsely populated beyond the main settlement at the eponymous Pulau Derawan. Most of the locals here are ethnic Bajau, the so-called "sea gypsies" of the past, who still carry on their lives very close to the water, albeit now in coastal villages rather than boats.

EASTERN KALIMANTAN: OIL TOWNS AND RIVER JOURNEYS

If you swing into Balikpapan, main entry point for East Kalimantan, expecting a sleepy pirate port on the edge of the jungle, you may be in for a shock. Cash from the surrounding oil fields has been flowing through the town for decades and today it's an outpost of striking sophistication by provincial Indonesian standards and a pleasant place to soak up a little luxury. But really Balikpapan is just a launch-pad for what lies beyond, and perhaps the most iconic Kalimantan adventure begins up the coast in Samarinda.

This town, the capital of East Kalimantan, is a far grittier place, dominated by a striking modern mosque. Samarinda marks the mouth of the mighty Mahakam, a 600-mile (965-km) thread of sediment-laden water running from hidden headwaters high in the Müller Range, the vast mountain system at the heart of Borneo. Journeys up this river, by public ferry in the lower reaches and by chartered speedboat or traditional dugouts in the upper stretches, are the stuff of travel legend, and as the river narrows the traditions of the Dayaks begin to show through the skin of Indonesian modernity. And if you want true adventure, you can always continue on foot once the canoes can travel no further, completing the grueling cross-Borneo trek over the Müller Range and down into the basin of the west-flowing Kapuas River, a journey many dream of but few have ever completed.

North of the Mahakam there are other rivers flowing though yet wilder country, homeland of some of the best-known Dayak groups, the Kenyah and the Punan. The Wehea Forest here is a true pristine wilderness, still home to sun bears, clouded leopards and orangutans.

ABOVE While Dayak groups across Kalimantan produce distinctive art, the Kenyah have some of the strongest decorative traditions of all. Images such as this one on a longhouse in the village of Mahak in East Kalimantan, originally represented ancestral spirits or deities. These days most Kenyah are Christian but older customs still inspire their arts. **LEFT** Seen from the cockpit of a helicopter, the scale of Kalimantan becomes apparent. Here the vast Mahakam delta unfolds below. The entire drainage basin of the Mahakam covers an area of 29,768 square miles (77,100 square km), while the distance from source to sea is around 600 miles (965 km). The river has long served as a conduit for trade. **RIGHT** Kalimantan is home to many species of pitcher plant. The jug-like structure which gives these plants their name is, in fact, a trap. Insects are attracted to the pitchers, which contain nectar. But once inside they find it difficult to escape thanks to the slippery, curved rim. The plant digests them and feeds off the nutrients.

Jungle Wanderers: The Dayaks

Few peoples have been more subjected to the force of exotic mythology by the outside world than the Dayaks of inner Borneo. Little more than a hundred years ago serious European authors were reporting that some of their number had tails, and even in the twenty-first century stories of headhunting raids, hornbill worship and unchanged hunter-gatherer lifestyles get heavy rotation amongst travel writers.

The term "Dayak" is actually a catchall for around 200 distinct groups whose traditional territories span the entire area of Borneo away from the narrow Malay-dominated coastal periphery. Tribal warfare, and indeed headhunting, were features of life for many Dayak groups in times past but most have long since settled down to living much like Indonesians elsewhere. Christianity has become the dominant religion in Dayak country, with smaller Muslim communities amalgamated with the coastal Malay population. Some, however, still cleave to older traditions, collectively known as *Kaharingan*.

LEFT A woman in the township of Long Bagun, on the banks of the Mahakam, displays her impressive ear piercings. The practice of ear stretching was once common amongst many Dayak groups. Girls would have their ears pierced at a young age and heavy rings or weights, usually made of brass, would be added over time to gradually stretch their lobes.

TOP The precise meaning of Dayak motifs, such as this one on a longhouse gable end, can be hard to discern but many draw on old beliefs that envisage the cosmos as an abstract "tree of life". One Dayak belief system, originally practiced by the Ngaju of Central Kalimantan and known as *Kaharingan*, has been recognized as a form of Hinduism, giving it status amongst Indonesia's officially sanctioned religions.

TOP RIGHT Although the Dayaks are linguistically and culturally diverse, speaking many languages and practicing many lifestyles, a strong sense of pan-Dayak identity has emerged within the modern Indonesian nation. Dayak performers regularly take part in major national arts events, such as this one in Java.

RIGHT While greatly improved road networks and ever more reliable air links have seen much passenger traffic shift from the river, the Mahakam is still a highway of sorts for cargo and short journeys.

SOUTH AND CENTRAL KALIMANTAN: "MEN OF THE FOREST"

Central Kalimantan is a vast province, stretching from the mangrove-meshed southern coastline northwards through the broad basins of the Barito, the Kahayan and the Mendawai and into the interlocking spurs of the Schwaner and Müller ranges. Most travelers, though, set their sights on one small coastal corner of the province, the thickly forested promontory of the Tanjung Puting National Park south of Kumai and Pangkalan Bun. This remarkable place is home to some 6,000 orangutans, the single largest population of these great apes anywhere in the wild.

The "man of the forest" is Asia's only great ape and it once roamed widely across Borneo and Sumatra, though decades of poaching and habitat loss have left it restricted to isolated pockets of surviving wilderness. While Sumatra's Bukit Lawang is the place for low-budget orangutan encounters, Tanjung Puting, reached via a flight to Pangkalan Bun, offers a more immersive experience thanks to the atmospheric inbound journey to the park aboard a *klotok* river boat. It's not all about orangutans here either. Unmistakable proboscis-nosed monkeys, found only in Borneo, graze in the thick forest canopies here, along with macaques and gibbons. Hornbills trace sweeping flight paths through the still air, and somewhere in the deeper shadows clouded leopards stalk.

The little province of South Kalimantan, occupying the southernmost angle of the island, is dwarfed by its neighbors. The slender range of the Meratus Mountains forms the spine of the region, while the huge city of Banjarmasin, squatting at the mouth of the Barito, is one of the biggest settlements in Borneo. It is every inch a river town, and its floating markets are a far cry from the sanitized tourist trap equivalents in Thailand and other parts of mainland Southeast Asia. Inland, meanwhile, the hill country around Loksado has cool, misty mornings, Dayak homestays and accessible jungle trails.

TOP Kalimantan is true orangutan territory. While the name of this great ape means "forest person" in Malay and Indonesian, traditionally it was more commonly known locally as *mawas*. Orangutans were once widespread across the whole of Borneo, though defor-estation for timber and the palm oil industry has seen their habitat become increasingly fragmented. Around 50,000 wild orangutans survive in both the Malaysian and Indonesian sections of the island. Tanjung Puting in Central Kalimantan is home to a significant population.
RIGHT The national park at Tanjung Puting in Central Kalimantan is famed for its population of around 6,000 orangutans. Many are rehabilitated former captives or orphans returned to the forest as part of a long-running program established here by Canadian primatologist Birutė Galdikas. Travelers can tour the park and visit the orangutan feeding stations aboard small boats like the one shown here.

ABOVE The Meratus Mountains around Loksado are craggy and thickly forested. They rise to around 6,000 feet (1,830 meters). Borneo is markedly less volcanic than the islands of Indonesia's main southern chain and these mountains are largely made up of sedimentary rocks originally laid down below the surface of the sea in the cretaceous period.

LEFT AND BELOW Each morning, shortly after dawn, long, low open boats begin to gather on the Martapura River, east of Banjarmasin. This is the Lok Baintan floating market. Unlike many other floating markets in countries such as Thailand and Cambodia, this is first and foremost a place of local commerce rather than a staged tourist attraction. As in more conventional markets on land, most of the vendors are women. Fresh produce dominates: fruit, vegetables, fish and meat. There are also little floating food stalls serving snacks, simple meals and coffee. Another floating market closer to the center of Banjarmasin has suffered from competition with more convenient shopping options ashore, but Lok Baintan still thrives.

WEST KALIMANTAN: CHINESE TOWNS AND FORGOTTEN RIVERS

The city of Pontianak straddles both the equator and the Kapuas River. It has the most sinister name of any city in Indonesia as a *pontianak* is a particularly malevolent ghost, the spirit of a woman who died in childbirth. The river mouth, it is rumored, was long haunted by legions of wicked *pontianaks* until an adventurer of Arab descent established a base here in the eighteenth century. The ghosts seem to have vanished but traces of a rakish past of piracy and immigration linger all along this coast, not least in the large ethnic Chinese population. Blood-red Buddhist and Confucian temples abound and, unusually for Indonesia, you'll sometimes hear Chinese languages spoken in the streets. The most Chinese of all towns is Singkawang, a faded throwback to a nineteenth-century gold rush, still peppered with shop-houses and temples and still full of the flavors of Chinese cuisine.

Inland, meanwhile, true adventure beckons along the Kapuas, Indonesia's longest river. This is not a destination for casual excursionists and travel here is far harder to organize than on the more navigable Mahakam further east. But those with sufficient time and toughness can find an authenticity here, upstream of the riverside settlement of Putussibau.

LEFT Pontianak's old-fashioned coffee houses, like the one shown here, are a reminder of the close proximity of Malaysia. As across the border, these *kopitiam* are a social institution. The name is a hybrid of the Malay and Indonesian word for coffee, *kopi*, and the Hokkien Chinese word *tiam*, meaning shop.

TOP Where it passes through Pontianak, the Kapuas is a broad channel. From here it runs back east for over 700 miles (1,125 km), making it the longest river in Indonesia. It rises in the central Müller Range and for centuries provided the only access from the coast to the Kapuas Hulu region.

Derawan: The Easy-going Archipelago

Like fragments of some shattered piece of green-gold porcelain, the tiny Derawan Archipelago is quite unlike the rest of Kalimantan. There are no seething river mouth ports or oil palm plantations here. Derawan, a 20-minute speedboat ride off the northern coast of East Kalimantan, is a castaway paradise comprising 31 specks of sand and greenery surrounded by clear waters and excellent diving conditions.

There's a low-key backpacker scene on the main island, Pulau Derawan, the sort of place where passers-by get stalled for many more weeks than they ever initially intended, and there are a handful of offshore dive resorts. But for the most part the islands seem barely inhabited and scarcely visited. Underwater, meanwhile, there are corals, sharks, manta rays and more.

ABOVE A fiery sunset over Derawan. Of the 31 isolated islands that make up this little archipelago, only two, Maratua and Derawan itself, are inhabited by small Bajau communities. The lack of human activity has kept the local seas pristine, a haven for green turtles (**TOP**) and many other species.

ABOVE Far inland from Pontianak lies the area known as Kapuas Hulu, "Upper Kapuas", centered on the riverside town of Putussibau seen here. Beyond the town this is a beautiful area seldom visited by tourists. Some fine longhouse communities stand upstream along the river and off the road that runs towards the Malaysian border. Also nearby is the stunning Danau Sentarum National Park, a vast network of islands, swamps and interconnecting lakes and channels, best explored by boat.

ABOVE Local transport in Kampung Beting, a stilt village on the outskirts of Pontianak. Settlements like this are typically dominated by the Malay-speaking Muslims who have lived along the coast for hundreds of years. It was usually from the Malay population that the royal houses of the Borneo littoral rose. The Pontianak sultanate was founded by Yemeni settlers who married into the Malay community down the decades.

THE IMPROBABLE ISLAND

Sulawesi dances on the face of the world like a demented dervish, spindly limbs flailing, scattering a confetti of small islets in all directions. Its crazed geography, with four distinct peninsulas jutting from a mountain- and lake-dappled fulcrum, creates space for jaw-dropping distance and diversity within a relatively small landmass. An overland journey from Makassar in the southwest to Manado in the northeast covers over 1,000 miles (1,610 km).

Sulawesi is a land in which green hills descend steeply to clear blue waters where the sunlight shines back in blinding stars from the steel domes of village mosques. Traditional Bugis schooners still make journeys under sail, and there are faded traces of pirate kingdoms out amongst the islets that trail into the Flores Sea.

The natural world here has profound peculiarities, borne of Sulawesi's improbable origins. The *anoa*, a miniature buffalo the size of a large dog, lives in the upland forests, as do *babirusa*, ferociously tusked wild pigs. There are slow-moving tarsiers with eyes like dinner plates and long-faced, Mohawk-sporting, black-crested macaques in the northern jungles. Underwater, meanwhile, there are some of the finest coral gardens in Asia. There's a similar diversity amongst the peoples of Sulawesi too, and the island is a patchwork of ethnicities, religions and languages.

LEFT Sunset at Selayar, off Sulawesi's southwest peninsula. An isolated backwater today, this long, narrow island was once an important trading center on old archipelago networks, with links to Java, Maluku and possibly even as far as Vietnam.

TOP Sulawesi's contribution to the maritime world is an elegant model of schooner, generically known as *pinisi*. Traditionally built on the beach at Bira, the interest of cruise operators in classic ships has reinvigorated old skills in recent years.

SOUTHWEST SULAWESI: THE FULCRUM OF THE INDONESIAN ARCHIPELIGO

The southwestern limb of Sulawesi has long been the fulcrum of maritime mastery in Indonesia. Today the city of Makassar is still the transit point for traffic between western and eastern regions. Its location at the very center of the archipelago allowed the local Bugis and Makassarese chiefs to attain great power over the sea lanes in centuries past, and even once the Dutch cowed the Makassar-based Gowa sultanate in the seventeenth century Bugis privateers remained a force to be reckoned with.

Today Makassar is a bustling seafront city, looking west towards flaming sunsets. The old Dutch stronghold of Fort Rotterdam, with its steep red roofs, is a reminder of the colonial past, and the extensive Chinese neighborhood tells of a history of trade and immigration. Makassar is also rightly famed for its seafood.

For most visitors Makassar is simply a way station for journeys to points north, but those who strike out to the south into the old Makassarese strongholds will find powdery white sands around

An Island of Many Parts

Geologically and ecologically Sulawesi is a Franken-stein's monster of an island, disparate limbs stitched together and given life by the power of plate tecton-ics. The shorter eastern arms of the island were orig-inally part of the southern supercontinent of Gondwa-naland. Traveling westwards on the deep convection currents of the earth's mantle, they ploughed into the midriff of the longer western section which originat-ed in the northern landmass of Laurasia. The impact buckled the island into its current contorted form. With one half from the Australian zone and the other from Asia, Sulawesi is still a place of strange fusion, home to both primates and marsupials.

Straddling ecological spheres as it does, Sulawesi has the quality of a strange Noah's Ark when it comes to wildlife, full of unexpected contrasts. There are clear links to neighboring Borneo, securely on the Asian side of the Wallace Line, when it comes to birdlife. The red-knobbed hornbill (**BELOW**) is unique to Sulawesi but it is closely related to the various other hornbill species of Borneo. However, an-other iconic Sulawesi bird, the maleo, is a megapode, closely related to Australian brush turkeys. Below the water there is a similar rich diversity, from huge manta rays to tiny porcelain crabs (**TOP**).

Bira. This is where many of Sulawesi's celebrated *pinisi* schooners were built in decades past. Still further south, Selayar and the coral-fringed Bone Rate Islands are miles from the beaten track.

The road north from Makassar is that which most travelers follow, past the turning to the Bantimurung waterfall in its spray-dampened, butterfly-crowded dell. The famed explorer-zoologist Alfred Russel Wallace came here hunting bugs in 1856. Onwards, the main road hugs the coast, warty karst outcrops rising inland over a narrow ledge of rice land until Pare Pare, where one route ploughs inland towards the fabled fastness of Tana Toraja, while a quieter route continues close to the coast to Polewali where a tortuous mountain road cuts north, twisting and turning to Mamasa, the wilder, less known sister region to Toraja.

TOP The gaze of the ancestors. Commemorative effigies, known as *tau-tau*, stare out from their cliff face niches at Lemo, a traditional burial site in Tana Toraja. Tombs are carved into the same cliff. **LEFT** Makassar's Fort Rotterdam was established as the center of Dutch power in eastern Indonesia after they defeated the powerful forces of southern Sulawesi in 1667. Today it is a well-preserved example of colonial architecture.

TANA TORAJA: AN UPLAND FASTNESS

Village houses stand in rows like moored schooners, their high prows angling upwards, their facades worked with worming patterns of black, ochre and white and their support pillars armored with the horns of countless buffalo. Nearby, in niches cut into a pale cliff, rank after rank of wide-eyed effigies stare out across a landscape of almost fluorescent greenery backed by dark hills.

Deep in the uplands at the heart of Sulawesi, Tana Toraja stands out even amidst Indonesia's exceptional array of traditional cultures. The architecture, the ceremonial traditions and the landscapes here rival the best that Bali has to offer, though with far fewer tourists.

It was the Muslim Bugis of the coast who first spoke of the animist people of the interior who had so stridently resisted their incursions as *to ri aja*, "people of the mountains". Dutch colonialists, who only reached this upland fastness in the early

TOP The remarkable *tongkonan* houses of Tana Toraja are the region's most obvious badge of identity. Torajan houses are steeped in ritual significance and symbolism. A *tongkonan* is an "origin house", through which members of an individual family can trace their lineage even if they no longer actually live there.

RIGHT Toraja funerals are sometimes delayed for months or even years, and in the interim the deceased is kept in the family home. When the funeral finally takes place, after elaborate preparations, it is accompanied by the sacrifice of many buffalo. The meat is then doled out to guests.

Toraja by the Back Door

Most people reach Tana Toraja aboard a bus from Makassar. But there is another option. A rough track winds through the hills between Mamasa and the town of Bittuang in the west of Toraja proper. It's an easy trek, with village homestays for overnight stops, usually taking two nights, though by hitching a motorbike ride on the early and later sections it's possible to complete with just one overnight stop. Along the way you'll pass through a misty landscape where alpine and tropical vegetation meet and mingle and where the *banau sura* houses of Mamasa shade slowly into the better known *tongkonan* of Toraja.

The tracks that thread their way through the green uplands of Mamasa form important links for outlying farming communities. Travelers undertaking the Mamasa-Toraja trek will often encounter locals heading for market along the trail (**TOP**). The route crosses a low pass east of Mamasa town, then descends to the little village of Timbaan, which makes a fine overnight stop. From here a rough track wends its way along steep hillsides to Ponding. The final stage crosses another saddle of high ground before the terraced landscapes of Toraja (**BELOW**) unfold ahead.

twentieth century, borrowed and modified the term and eventually the locals embraced it themselves and made it a proud badge of identity. Today almost all Torajans are Christian. But the older, ancestor-venerating *Aluk Todolo* belief system has endured as a current of *adat*, "custom", alongside the church. It still governs many aspects of life and, more importantly, death, not least in the form of the famed Torajan funerals mostly held during the dry months of July and August, with their wild feasting and bloody buffalo sacrifice.

The hub of Tana Toraja is the riverside market town of Rantepao, and this is a fine base for excursions to nearby villages with their distinctive *tongkonan* houses and cliff burials with *tau-tau* effigies. But it's easy to get deeper into the countryside, either with your own transport or by hitching rides in battered local minibuses. The village of Batutumongga, high on the flanks of Mount Sesran, has a clutch of simple guest houses, places that often float above a vast inverted cloudscape in the liquid gold of a Torajan dawn.

TOP Torajan *tongkonan* houses are often intricately decorated in black, white and ochre. Modernity has done little to diminish these artistic expressions and, in fact, the more modern houses are often amongst the most lavishly decorated, a sign of increasing prosperity and enduring cultural pride. The decorative elements are mostly abstract though they often feature important symbolic elements. Buffalos, the ultimate Torajan motif, almost always appear somewhere.

THE CENTER OF SULAWESI

The sprawling province of Central Sulawesi embraces the gaping inlet of Teluk Tomini like a pair of green arms. For years this was one of those unfortunate corners of Indonesia that foreign government travel advisories urged travelers to avoid. The source of the trouble was a bitter communal conflict between local Christians and Muslims around Poso. Today peace has returned and the region is back on the travel map, and while most visitors head helter-skelter for the offshore Togians, the mainland has plenty to offer too.

Danau Poso is a breezy body of water at the very center of Sulawesi, with clove plantation-covered hills sloping down to glass-clear waters, hemmed with thin yellow beaches. Sleepy Tentena, with its white churches and nearby waterfalls, is the best base here.

Northwest of the lake is Central Sulawesi's great wilderness. The mellifluously named Lore Lindu National Park spans a tranche of the complicated mountain landscape that fills the central hinterland of the island. Far from major population centers, it is a true wild space, crisscrossed by only a few tenuous trails. There are tarsiers, endangered Tonkean macaques, cuscus and other beasts found only in Sulawesi at large here. The easiest access is along the parched Palu Valley, south of the regional capital, but you can also travel from Danau Poso to the Bada Valley on the southern edge of the park, a beautiful area where striking carved megaliths rise from the fields like Indonesian cousins of the famed Easter Island heads.

ABOVE Set at the northern tip of Lake Poso, the friendly town of Tentena is a place of well-tended gardens and cool breezes. The surrounding hills are thickly forested and coursed by many waterfalls, such as the one seen here. There are also some excellent beaches on the shores of the lake, especially that at Siuri, which has golden sand and clean water. Eels, caught in bamboo traps in the lake, are a Tentena delicacy.

BELOW In a tranquil setting on the outskirts of Tentena in Central Sulawesi stand the spectacular bamboo structures of the Mosintuwu Institute. Founded by local activist Lian Gogali, the institute works to promote harmony in a region formerly troubled by sectarian conflict through women's empowerment and education. It's an inspirational place, which also welcomes curious visitors to its library and lakeside café.

The Togian Islands

The long northern arms of Sulawesi enclose the Togian Islands like the most precious of secrets. This little archipelago takes considerable effort to access by ferry from either Gorontalo or from Ampana, northeast of Poso. But it's a journey well worth taking. There are deliciously low-key dive resorts and budget beach bungalows in a few spots, magnificent diving and snorkeling, pretty little fishing hamlets and sandy trails striking out into the deeply forested interiors. There's every reason to linger here a little longer than you originally intended and that's what many people end up doing.

The Togians offer some superb diving. The reefs are in excellent condition and the waters are crystal clear. Snorkelers also get to share in the action, with plenty of shallow, accessible sites. The spot known as California Reef is particularly impressive, a great hulk of coral rising from the depths far from shore. Clown fish (**ABOVE MIDDLE**) are just one of the many residents. Delicate sun corals (**ABOVE**) can also be spotted in the clear waters around the Togians.

TOP Dusk falls on the Togians. The islands sit in the middle of Teluk Tomini, the great bay formed by Sulawesi's northernmost arms. They are sparsely populated, with rugged interiors. The low-key tourist developments and local communities cling to the coast, with boats the main means of transport, even between settlements on the same island. The islands have been settled by many different groups over the years, including Bajau and Pamona people.

ABOVE Tourism in the Togians has remained low-key thanks in part to the effort required to get there. Isolated bungalow complexes and modest dive resorts are marooned around the coasts, most of them accessible only by boat. Many stand in splendid isolation, though there is a little clutch of places together on Kadidiri, shown here, a small island close to Wakai, the main settlement in the archipelago.

OUT ON A LIMB: NORTHERN SULAWESI

Northern Sulawesi is out on a limb, a slender arm stretching eastwards then ending with a delicate flick, which seems to whip a dusting of tiny islands upwards towards the Philippines. The rest of Indonesia feels a very long way away. Formerly a single province, it is now split between Gorontalo and North Sulawesi, with its capital at Manado. The whole region is a place of rearing green mountains, surpassing 6,000 feet (1,830 meters) on their highest ridges and then plunging precipitously to cobalt-colored waters.

Manado is the main gateway here, with the prime attractions right on its doorstep, and most visitors fly straight in from other parts of Indonesia or even from Singapore or Malaysia. At the utmost ends of the Indonesian earth, Manado was long a staging post for foreign seafarers. Spanish and Portuguese travelers came here and planted the first seeds of Christianity amongst the palm trees in the sixteenth century. Later, Dutch missionaries took over and today the town is still a place of whitewashed churches and Sunday choirs. Manado is a pleasant, modern city, but the main attractions lie beyond, beneath the clear blue waters to the north or in the cool green Minahasan highlands to the south.

For many people the Manado region is synonymous with diving, for just a short boat ride from the city is the Bunaken National Park, dominated by the towering volcanic island of

TOP Bunaken is just a short boat ride from busy Manado, with its traffic and shopping malls. But it is worlds apart, a coral-hemmed dot of land surrounded by clear, clean waters. It has long been a favorite dive destination.

ABOVE MIDDLE On the other side of the lens, an underwater photographer looks for the perfect angle on the marine life of Bunaken. The water drops away steeply beyond the island's fringing reef, and the nutrient-rich upwellings keep the coral healthy. **ABOVE** A common lionfish cruises its patch of reef. These fierce-looking predatory fish have poisonous spines, which protect them from larger sea creatures. They are not aggressive but are best avoided as their sting is extremely painful.

The Wild Southeast

The province of Southeast Sulawesi, across the deep bight of Teluk Bone, rarely makes it onto travelers' itineraries, lying as it does so very far from major transport hubs. But stretching from its southernmost shoreline are a scattering of small islands which draw divers from far and wide. The Wakatobi Marine National Park surrounds Kepulauan Tukangbesi, literally the "Blacksmith Islands", a hint at Sulawesi's historical association with iron and bronze production. There are a few isolated dive resorts here, endless empty beaches, and beneath the surface mile upon mile of reefs in a fine state of preservation.

Manado Tua. Pulau Bunaken itself is the main island accommodation center, with easy access to crystalline waters and plunging drop-offs. On the other side of the peninsula there is a very different underwater world in the prized muck diving around Pulau Lembeh. There are also new submarine frontiers opening up amongst the islands that stretch northwards from Sulawesi.

Ashore, meanwhile, the Minahasan heartlands have breezy mountain lakes, the shattered form of the Gunung Lokon volcano to climb, and the notoriously gruesome market at Tomohon where they seem to consider just about every creature under the sun fair game. But the real dry land treasure of North Sulawesi is the otherworldly forest of the Tangkoko Batuangus Nature Reserve, the most accessible of all Sulawesi's wilderness areas.

The clear waters of Wakatobi are rich with marine life, from lividly colored pink dor: ID nudibranchs (**LEFT**), a kind of soft-shelled mollusk, and slow-moving cuttlefish (**TOP**) to green sea turtles (**BELOW**) and hawksbills, which nest on the islands.

ABOVE The black-crested macaques of the Tangkoko Batuangus reserve in northern Sulawesi are one of the island's best-known species thanks in part for their willingness to pose for photos. They live in groups and forage on the forest floor. **TOP** A snorkeler explores the underwater worlds off Manado, with the unmistakable outline of Manado Tua in the distance. This dormant volcano rises straight out of the sea alongside the low island of Bunaken, the main diving center.

THE FABLED SPICE ISLANDS

An infinity of islands swirling like wind-blown petals across the map, all sense of geographical order seems finally to break down in Maluku. This is where Indonesia's archipelagic character reaches its apogee. There are around a thousand individual islands here, a lifetime of landfalls, riding in the stream of history.

In Maluku the past comes richly spiced. For the freebooting merchant adventurers of old these were the Spice Islands, the only place on earth to find nutmeg and cloves. The astronomical value of these obscure condiments drew in Arabs, Portuguese, Hollanders and Englishmen, and in the seventeenth century Maluku was the stage on which the opening acts of European imperialism were played out.

Today there's still a faint whiff off cloves pervading the sleepy streets of Ternate and Tidore and a hint of nutmeg on the warm winds of Banda. But Maluku has slipped back into sweet obscurity, only the moldering fortifications and rusting cannon here and there to show that much blood was spilt in the name of the spice trade hereabouts.

For travelers Maluku is an island-hopping extravaganza. Improved air transport links with western Indonesia have made flying visits to the major destinations increasingly practical. But for the most part this is still a region of new frontiers, with a sense that the topmasts of the seventeenth-century merchant ships have only just dropped below the horizon.

ABOVE The ultimate Malukan spice: freshly harvested nutmeg, with the red seed covering that is dried and sold as mace.

LEFT The waters at Sawai, a fishing village on the north coast of Seram, are as clear as glass. The interior of Seram is hard to access but coastal spots like Sawai attract a few visitors.

RIGHT The tiny Banda island of Run in the fresh light of morning. This pinprick of land was swapped by the British in 1667 for another small island, Manhattan, up until that point claimed by the Dutch.

BELOW Sawai's little fishing community is built directly over the water on stilts and backed by steep cliffs. There is accommodation for visitors here in one of Maluku's most memorable locations.

AMBON & AROUND: THE HEART OF MALUKU

Ambon, at the heart of Maluku, is what passes for a metropolis amongst the fractured landfalls of eastern Indonesia, but it is still worlds away from the big cities of Java. Steamy, palm-clad hills rise just beyond the southernmost suburbs, and the sheltered waters of the bay are busy with boats from distant harbors. Most visitors simply touch base here then head on to other islands. But for divers Ambon itself is a prized destination. There are dive resorts around the island and a diverse range of dive sites just offshore.

East of Ambon Island are the Lease Islands, Haruku, Saparua and Nusa Laut, sleepy, leafy places visited by only a handful of tourists. The islands of central Maluku were influenced in equal measure by the Muslim sultans of Ternate to the north and by the enthusiastically proselytizing Portuguese merchants, and today the population is a patchwork of Muslim and Christian communities, with mosques and churches rising amongst the palms.

All of these islands are overshadowed by the long hulk of Seram, rising darkly to the north. In traditional Malukan belief this is *Nusa Ina*, the "Mother Island", place of ancestral origin. A towering ridge of mountains runs the length of the island, almost 10,000 feet (3,050 meters) at the highest summits and thickly swathed with jungle on the lower slopes. Neither Islam nor Christianity made much headway here in the interior in centuries past and until very recently indigenous belief systems had a stronghold. There were reports of headhunting in the forests of Seram little more than half a century ago, and even today the place has an ominous reputation for sorcery. Some of the indigenous groups, known collectively as Alfur, are rumored to possess the gifts of invincibility and flight. The Nuaulu, with their distinctive red bandanas, are the most traditional of the Alfur peoples, though meeting them, and indeed doing any sort of exploration in inner Seram, is no easy thing. This, like so many other parts of Maluku, is a place where tourism and exploration are one and the same.

TOP LEFT The north coast of Seram, particularly the beautiful Sawai Bay area, has begun to sprout idyllic little resort hideaways in recent years, some with accommodation built to mimic the traditional stilt villages that dot the area.
LEFT There is excellent diving in many corners of Maluku. The underwater adventures begin just a short hop from the region's main gateway, Ambon, where there are great dive sites off the coast.
RIGHT A young man from Ambon demonstrates the *Cakalele* dance. This ritual war dance, featuring participants wielding swords and spears, is performed across Maluku. It is particularly associated with Ambon, a place proud of its martial past and especially of the 1817 revolt against Dutch forces led by Thomas Matulessy, better known as Pattimura, after whom Ambon's airport is named.

Maluku's Deep South: The Edge of the Map

In the southern reaches of Maluku the map seems to come to pieces. Blue distance expands out of all normal proportion, with sudden turquoise blotches showing here and there, atolls that may rear above sea level to form yet another desert island or which may not manage to break the surface at all, leaving nothing but the haunting outline of an island that never was. Maluku's trademark muddle of Muslim and Christian communities continues in the south, but older belief systems are closer to the surface than anywhere else and strange tales of magic hexes and supernatural powers abound.

Southern Maluku is, for the most part, true adventure territory, miles from even the most adventurous tourist itineraries. In recent years, however, one archipelago within an archipelago here has begun to register as a faint blip on the travel radar. An offbeat alternative to the Bandas, the Kei Islands, sometimes also spelt "Kai", have a very strong claim to having the

very best beaches in the whole of Indonesia, with miles of powdery sands as white as sugar and as fine as flour. There are flights to Kei Kecil from Ambon and a handful of lonely beach bungalow operations for those looking for a real castaway experience.

The other island groups here float in an ocean of dreams. The jumble of Aru rises from the shelf of shallows off the southwest coast of Papua. This was once a trading outpost where Chinese and Bugis merchants came to gather all the outlandish produce of this edge of the world zone: pearls from Tanimbar, sea cucumbers from the northern edge of Australia and the feathers of the fabulous birds of paradise that shimmered like spun silver in the branches of the interior. The Tanimbar Islands lie further west, with their lingering megalithic culture. Still further west, a string of small landfalls run towards the easternmost tail of Nusa Tenggara: Babar, Leti, Damar, Wetar and other names to conjure with.

ABOVE A man enjoys a moment of splendid isolation amidst craggy limestone and turquoise seas in the Kei Islands. Despite their remoteness, the Keis have long been tied into networks of interisland trade and immigration. The original inhabitants belonged to the Melanesian ethnic group that dominates most of southern Maluku. But over the centuries many settlers arrived from other parts of the archipelago, creating an ethnic melting pot. The local aristocracy, known as the Mel-Mel, claim to be descended from Balinese adventurers who arrived in the distant past.

ABOVE The Kei Islands, an isolated cluster of low-lying islands in the southeast of Maluku, feature powdery white sand, palm trees and all the other desert island requisites. They also have a fascinating culture, with strong *adat* traditions running alongside the majority Christian faith, especially in the southernmost island of Tanimbar-Kei.

RIGHT A galaxy of starfish on the shore in the Kei Islands. Commonly known as the chocolate chip sea star, for obvious reasons, these *Protoreaster nodosus* starfish are common throughout Indonesian waters. They usually live in sandy shallows rather than on reefs and are easily spotted by snorkelers. The warm, clear waters off the Keis are home to a wealth of marine life.

BANDA: THE NUTMEG ISLANDS

A cluster of miniscule pinpricks on the broad face of the sea south of Seram, the Banda Islands scarcely make it onto the map. A 12-hour ferry ride or a sketchily scheduled hop in a twin-prop aircraft from Ambon, they are as small and as remote as Indonesian islands come. There are just seven inhabited islands here, most of them less than a mile across. Traffic is mainly made up of a few rattling pedicabs and the odd flock of wayward chickens. The little townships seem to be on the brink of being swamped by the rampant tropical greenery that seeps down from the hills inland. People move slowly here but smile quickly.

And yet, improbable as it may seem, this forgotten archipelago was once the focus of fierce passions. It was, in fact, the kernel from which the whole sprawling edifice of European empire in Southeast Asia sprouted, for the Bandas were once the world's one and only source of the most precious of all spices: nutmeg.

TOP The Bandas are gloriously tranquil today but they have a decid-edly bloody history. The centuries-long struggle for control of the nutmeg business between the Dutch, the British and the local chiefs known as *Orang Kaya*, literally "Rich Men", saw atrocities committed by all sides, most notoriously the 1621 massacre by Dutch forces of all but a handful of the indigenous inhabitants. **LEFT** Thanks to their unique past as the ultimate wellspring of the world spice industry and a fulcrum around which global history turned during the early years of European involvement in Asia, the Bandas have a proud cultural identity. Here local women perform a traditional dance in Banda-neira, the capital of the archipelago.

For many centuries the trade in this fragrant nut into the western hemisphere was carefully controlled by Arab middlemen and their trading partners in Venice. But from the sixteenth century first Portuguese, then Dutch and British sailors tussled furiously for exclusive control of this unimaginably lucrative crop. Today the legacy of this period is still plain to see amongst the moldering fortresses that stud the islands and in the shabbily dignified houses of the tiny capital, Bandaneira, with their Dutch-style roofs and deep verandas. And nutmeg still grows here in deep groves, shaded by taller stands of candlenut trees.

For travelers the Bandas are the most prized destination in Maluku. This is a place to linger for days and weeks, breathing deeply on the intoxicating air of island lethargy. There is homely accommodation in Bandaneira and a handful of other homestays on other islands, in particular Pulau Ai, which lies to the west. The diving around Banda ranks with Indonesia's best, with dramatic drop-offs and pristine corals.

BELOW Far from any other land, the ten little islets that make up the Bandas exist thanks to volcanic activity forcing up material from beneath the earth's crust to create this small archipelago. The cone-shaped Gunung Api seen here is currently dormant, but its eruptions have often troubled the people of the islands, most recently in 1988.

TOP RIGHT Fort Belgica, still presiding over Bandaneira, is the most dramatic relic of the long years of European involvement in the Bandas. Built in 1611, it replaced the older Fort Nassau, lower down the hillside, which itself was built over the ruins of a Portuguese outpost; the Portuguese were the first Europeans to reach the islands, in the sixteenth century.

ABOVE MIDDLE The Bandas are justly famous for their diving, with dramatic drop-offs and shallow coral gardens, all in excellent condition and teeming with fish. There's good snorkeling here too, especially off Hatta and Ai islands. There are a number of dive centers on the islands, and the Bandas also form a key stop on the itineraries of live-aboard dive boats.

ABOVE It's hard to imagine the days when nutmeg made the Bandas the most prized islands on earth. Back in the early seventeenth century the spice was worth more than gold by weight. It's not quite so valuable these days but there's still a nutmeg industry here, with the nuts dried and offered to buyers outside family homes in Bandaneira.

NORTHERN MALUKU: THE ISLANDS OF KINGS

When the first Arab seafarers reached Indonesia's Spice Islands sometime around the twelfth century, the sheer number of local chieftains made their heads spin. Virtually every speck of soil in these crowded seas had its own self-styled king with imperial ambitions. They called the place *Jazirat al-Muluk*, the "Islands of Kings", for there seemed to be almost as many sovereigns as spices. The name stuck, hence "Maluku". It was in the north that the most powerful of all Malukan royals emerged in the centuries after the arrival of Islam, and the two rival sultanates of Ternate and Tidore once had power and influence that far outstripped their tiny island seats.

Today Ternate is still the hub of North Maluku, though the provincial capital is now the overgrown village of Sofifi on the larger Halmahera Island. Ternate is a cone-shaped island, a volcano rising straight from the depths, still the seat of a sultan and still marked by the fortifications of the Portuguese and Dutch who once wrestled for control here. It is a sleepy place, though you can catch the scent of the past on the hot and hum: ID air. Hereabouts that past smells of cloves, for while Banda was the original source of nutmeg it was on Ternate that cloves were to be found as they still are today. Just across the water, Tidore exists in a state of supreme tropical torpor, its former kingly rivalry with Ternate seemingly forgotten.

ABOVE Local boys from Jailolo peering to see what lies beneath. Set at the foot of a perfectly formed volcanic peak on the west coast of Halmahera, Jailolo was once the seat of an independent sultanate. However, it frequently played the role of pawn in the Ternate-Tidore power struggles. Though Jailolo's rulers were often overthrown or exiled, the royal line somehow survived and a reigning sultan still lives in the town, though without official power. **OPPOSITE TOP** Seen from the south coast of Ternate, historical arch-rival Tidore rises in the dawn, with the smaller island of Maitara rising closer at hand. All the islands here are volcanic. **BELOW** Local children at Morotai enjoy beach life. During the Allied retaking of the Pacific during World War II, Morotai was used as a base for the US bombing of Japanese-occupied Manila.

Both islands are massively overshadowed by Halmahera, which rises to the east. A craggy green hulk with a tormented outline echoing that of the much larger Sulawesi to the west, Halmahera is another of Maluku's travel frontiers, rarely visited by travelers. For now there are a handful of hideaways in the north of the island, around Tobelo, which is also the jumping-off point for visits to Pulau Morotai where traces of the Allied occupation during the pushback against Japanese forces at the end of World War II are still rusting beneath the palms.

BELOW Sunset over Bacan. This cluster of islands off the southern peninsula of Halmahera is way off the beaten tourist track. The main island was the seat of another of North Maluku's feuding sultanates and a sultan still reigns here. The islands are thickly forested, and the sparse local population is made up of the descendants of settlers from many places around eastern Indonesia. There are non-human immigrants here too. The main island is home to troupes of black-crested macaques, which must have been introduced at some point from their native territory in northern Sulawesi.

RIGHT Cooking up a feast of fresh sardines at Jailolo. Though fishing is an important source of income here, Jailolo is mainly an agricultural community. Traditional festivities mark the rice harvest in August.

BELOW Children from Ternate learn the tricks of traditional weaving literally at their mothers' knees. Although northern Maluku does not have the strong cloth-making traditions found further south, thanks to Ternate's illustrious past it has attracted settlers from around eastern Indonesia, some of whom have brought their own weaving skills to the island. These women are preparing the colored yarn that will later be placed on the loom.

BEYOND THE SUNRISE

Papua is like nowhere else in Indonesia or on earth. Occupying the western half of New Guinea, it is vast beyond even Indonesia's unsurpassed concepts of vastness, an Australasian interloper thrusting its long neck deep into the eastern waters of the archipelago.

This is a place where tiny twin-prop planes labor through the turbulence between the cloud forest and the thunderheads to reach rough landing strips carved out of mountainsides a lifetime away from metaled roads and mains electricity. It is virgin territory for missionaries and miners, and for the Indonesian nation-state too. The Dutch clung on here long after the rest of Indonesia gained independence, only relinquishing control under international pressure in the early 1960s, by which time there was an insurmountable gulf between Indonesian national ambitions and the aspirations of many Papuans.

Today there is still much local disquiet at the region's heavy-handed absorption into Indonesia, and Papua is a frontier in every sense. For travelers though, it is a thrilling prospect, a place where even a package tour can feel like a pioneering expedition.

RIGHT Asmat country is low-lying and swampy, coursed by the many rivers that run south from the central mountain ranges to the Arafura Sea. The terrain makes for difficult access, which has kept the countryside relatively well preserved. **OPPOSITE BOTTOM** An Asmat elder poses outside the *jeu*. These long, partitioned "men's houses", built on stilts, are the traditional fulcrum of masculine Asmat society. Each village has its own *jeu*, some up to 300 feet (90 meters) long, with a door and fireplace for each sub-clan in the community. Traditionally unmarried young men slept in the *jeu* following initiation rites to mark the end of adolescence. All male villagers would gather in them for rituals, to discuss community affairs and to plan for war. **BELOW** Asmat men demonstrate their formidable canoeing prowess. Though generally only used for show these days, dugout canoes paddled at great speed by a party of standing men were the key vehicle for Asmat war parties in the past. The network of river channels allowed raiders to travel rapidly over long distances in this swampy region.

BEYOND THE BIRD'S HEAD: RAJA AMPAT

The westernmost promontory of Papua rears up towards the equator. The Dutch, gazing at the green cloud patterns of the atlas, called this huge headland the *Vogelkop*, the "Bird's Head". Large swathes of the river-cut southern lowlands of the Bird's Head have never been traversed by outsiders, and there may still be nomadic communities here who avoid all contact with the outside world. Papua is one of the only places outside of the Amazon basin where such peoples still survive.

The wilderness of the interior is a striking contrast with the city of Sorong on the western coast of the peninsula, a busy town fueled by oil money. There's a well-served airport here, which makes Sorong the natural gateway for the watery wonderland that begins a short way offshore. Just a few years ago the sparsely populated archipelago of well over a thousand limestone islands that stretches westwards from Sorong was exceptionally difficult to reach and completely devoid of facilities. Today though it is one of the hottest travel properties in Indonesia. The very mention of its name is enough to send globe-trotting divers and snorkelers into a trance: Raja Ampat.

The best-known dive sites and the resorts that serve them are located to the north and south of the Dampier Strait, named for the English pirate-explorer William Dampier who passed this way in the late seventeenth century. The waters are as clear as glass and swarming with staggering numbers of fish species, underwater cyclones of shimmering color. This is one of the finest venues for live-aboard diving excursions in Asia, while in recent years locals in the scattered fishing communities have started opening homestays, giving budget travelers a chance to visit Raja Ampat.

LEFT The karst limestone outcrops of the Fam Islands in Raja Ampat have become the most photographed place in Papua in recent years. The real attractions here, however, lie below the surface in what is one of the world's most prized diving destinations.

TOP Fish swarm over pristine coral in the clear waters off Gam, one of the central islands in the Raja Ampat archipelago. There are a number of villages here and plenty of homestay accommodation for visitors wanting to stay outside the dive resorts.

The Forbidding Asmat Swamplands

South of Papua's great central mountain ridge the land angles gently towards the turbid shallows of the Aru Sea, giving way uneasily to a swampy tangle of tidal inlets and muddy rivers bending between fence-like thickets of estuarine forest. It's a forbidding, unsettling world, seemingly caught between the land and the water, and it's the home of one of the most far-famed of all Papua's peoples: the Asmat. For early explorers the Asmat were the very epitome of tribal ferocity. With a tendency to come roaring out of hidden inlets in blade-like war canoes, their reputation for cannibalism was not, by any means, unfounded. These days, however, their fame rests instead on their exceptional traditional carving skills. Asmat art is prized by collectors worldwide.

The Asmat country is still tricky to visit. The stilt-built township of Agats has air connections to Merauke and is the base for guided trips up winding rivers to woodcarving communities further inland. Still deeper inland, many days travel upriver, is the homeland of the Korowai, one of the most staunchly traditional parts of all Papua, where a handful of family groups still live in their remarkable tree dwellings, full-size houses suspended in the branches.

ABOVE The Korowai people are best known for their elevated treehouse dwellings, perched high above the forest floor. Most Korowai now live in villages at ground level, though they still construct treehouses.

ABOVE Korowai men at ease in a treehouse. Although dramatically elevated houses have been built for show in recent years, traditional dwellings were usually much closer to ground level. **BELOW** Asmat men in full traditional regalia. Although it is sometimes claimed that the Asmat were cut off from outside contact until the twentieth century, they never lived in total isolation. They traded with people in other regions, including with inland people who provided them with stones for tools and weapons, unavailable in their muddy, marshy homeland.

ABOVE A Korowai man strikes a pose with bow and arrow. Traditionally the Korowai combined a hunter-gatherer lifestyle with shifting agriculture, living in settled communities and clearing forest gardens, but also gathering wild food from the forest.

CENDERAWASIH BAY AND THE BACK OF THE BIRD'S HEAD

The back of the Bird's Head Peninsula frames the eastern shore of Cenderawasih Bay, a chunk bitten out of the back of Papua. Manokwari, close to the northwestern corner of the bay, is the capital of West Papua province. From here excursions into the high, thickly forested Arfak Mountains are possible, a wild region where there's a chance of glimpses of birds of paradise along with visits to stilt villages.

Offshore, the waters of Cenderawasih Bay are a national park, speckled with small islands. Nabire, at the innermost point of the bay, is one of the best places on earth to encounter whale sharks. Standing sentinel across the mouth of the bay, meanwhile, are a clutch of bigger islands: Yapen, Numfor and Biak.

Biak is a destination in its own right, with good air connections from cities to the west. There's a dreamy island atmosphere here along the sandy lanes and powdery shorelines. The people of Biak have long been seafarers, with much more experience of passing outsiders than the Papuans of the mainland interior. Most traumatic of those encounters came during the Japanese occupation and subsequent Allied pushback of World War II. There are traces of the battles fought here in tunnel hideouts and crumbling gun emplacements. Biak faces northwards out onto the great blue yonder, a Pacific outrider in a nation which mostly looks instead towards the Indian Ocean. This coast, open to the full force of Pacific groundswells, is now being scouted out by surfers looking to escape the well-trammeled wave-riders' routes on the other side of the archipelago.

ABOVE In the clear blue waters of Cenderawasih Bay, off Nabire, a free-diver has a close encounter with a whale shark, attended by a school of remoras, sucker fish which hitch a ride on larger marine species. Whale sharks are the world's largest fish. They feed entirely on plankton and are relatively common in Indonesia.

BELOW A sailing ship, built along the lines of the traditional *pinisi* schooners of Sulawesi, rides at anchor off Manokwari. Inland, the thickly forested mountains of the Bird's Head Peninsula show through the clouds. The Arfak range is close to Manokwari and is a stronghold of traditional Papuan culture and is also rich in birdlife.

BELOW A Biak fisherman traverses the shallows near the village of Mnurwar. Biak was traditionally home to seafarers, enjoying better connections with the rest of the archipelago than much of mainland Papua. It was a vassal of the Tidore sultanate of Maluku for many centuries, though there was little effort to convert the island to Islam and it retained its traditional belief systems until the later arrival of Christianity. The former Indonesian name for the whole region, Irian, is in fact a Biak word, meaning something along the lines of "land rising from the sea".

Merauke and Beyond: To the Ends of the Earth

"From Sabang to Merauke" Indonesians say when they want to evoke the entire breadth of their enormous homeland, placing the extreme poles of the nation at Sabang, off the northernmost tip of Sumatra, and at Merauke, here in the steamy, swampy southeastern lowlands of Papua. For a place at the ends of the Indonesian earth, Merauke is actually a surprisingly modern and orderly town, with good flight connections. A tiny handful of travelers come here en route for excursions into the vast Wasur National Park, which stretches from the banks of the Maro River to the Papua New Guinea border.

ABOVE A lonely sunset on the coast near Merauke. Though Merauke town itself is a fairly sophisticated place, it is wildly remote, far closer to Australia and, of course, Papua New Guinea than any major Indonesian city.

LEFT Day's end at Inggiri, a short way west of Kota Biak, the main settlement on Biak. Today Christianity is the dominant religion on Biak, but in the mid-twentieth century a series of messianic movements known as *Koreri* emerged here.

BELOW There are excellent beaches all around the coast of Biak. Those along the southern shore are mostly sheltered, with calm waters and much coral offshore. The northwest coast, facing the Pacific, gets seasonal surf.

Jayapura: An Outpost of the Far East

Tucked into a mountain-sheltered bay just 30 miles (48 km) west of the Papua New Guinea border, Jayapura, capital of Papua province, is an impossibly far-flung outpost of mainstream Indonesia. There are tin-roofed mosques and Madurese *sate* hawkers, Padang-style food served up over plates of imported Javanese rice, and cargo ships registered to ports in sight of Singapore anchored off the seafront. This was once the Dutch center of operations, Hollandia. Today it's the main entry point for adventures in the mountain hinterland, with connections to Jakarta and Bali and onward flights to Wamena in the Baliem Valley as well as to all other major centers around Papua.

It's worth lingering a day or two here if time allows. There are some pleasant beaches nearby, deserted on weekdays and with reasonable surfing conditions at times. More enticing is the long, slender sheet of Danau Sentani. Jayapura's airport lies on the northern shores of this freshwater lake, but its stilt villages still feel a long way from the jet age. Close to both the lake and the airport, the growing modern town of Sentani is a good alternative base to Jayapura itself for those passing through by air.

THE BALIEM VALLEY: A LOST WORLD

High in the heartlands of Papua, beneath the great wall of the Jayawijaya Range with its seemingly impossible ice-capped 15,000-foot (4,570-meter) summits barely 300 miles (480 km) south of the equator, lies a locked world. This is the Baliem Valley, stronghold of the Dani people and the stuff of explorers' legend.

On a bright June day in 1938 an American pilot by the name of Richard Archbold came winging his way over the central mountains of Papua in a rattletrap seaplane. He was on an early reconnaissance mission for a planned exploration of these uplands, and the last thing he expected to see as he peered out of the cockpit was a vast patchwork of irrigated fields and round-roofed houses. Archbold had stumbled upon an advanced agricultural civilization about which the outside world knew absolutely nothing.

In the eight decades since that accidental discovery, much has changed in Baliem, not least the almost universal adoption of Christianity under the fervent influence of Dutch and American missionaries, and the arrival of modern Indonesian governance. More uncomplicatedly positive has been the general cessation of tribal violence which was once very much a part of daily life amongst the Dani, one of the most warlike of all Papua's societies.

Today travelers make use of the air link from Jayapura to Wamena, the valley capital, a peculiar grid of streets 5,400 feet (1,370 meters) above sea level and seemingly belonging to modern Indonesia but for the occasional striking sight of a Dani man dressed in little more than a traditional penis gourd rubbing shoulders in the streets with migrants from western Indonesia in standard skullcaps and headscarves.

A more unadulterated Dani world lies just beyond town in communities of thatched *honai* houses. But to get the very finest that the valley has to offer, the best bet is to set out on a trek along the trails between outlying villages, or even over the valley's eastern mountain walls into the wilder neighboring territories of the Yali people.

LEFT Children from a coastal suburb in Jayapura enjoy the view from the local jetty. Jayapura is the most diverse and cosmopolitan settlement in Papua and the most obviously "Indonesian". Much of its population is made up of settlers who have arrived from other parts of the archipelago over the last hundred years. There are large numbers of Javanese and people from Sulawesi, attracted by the economic opportunities of a growing regional capital. Islam has a stronger presence than elsewhere in Papua. There are also a few Balinese Hindus and a good number of Chinese Indonesians and indigenous Papuans.

TOP LEFT Jayapura is a city that has gone through many incarnations since it was founded a little more than a century ago. Although the coast here had long been visited by Bugis and Chinese traders and was, of course, home to plenty of local people, no significant port developed. A Dutch ship stopped by in 1858, but it was only in 1910 that the colonial settlement of Hollandia was established. After Papua became part of Indonesia, the name changed to Kota Baru, "New City", then briefly to Sukarnopura after the then president, before finally assuming its current name. Locals often know it as Port Numbay.

LEFT A group of Dani women and children practice their spear-throwing skills. The Dani are often described as "warlike", and conflicts were once common here. However, in traditional society clashes between villages were actually heavily ritualized and controlled, rarely giving way to actual warfare.

BELOW LEFT MIDDLE The next generation: a young Dani child in the Baliem Valley. The Dani are one of the best known of Papua's cultural groups. They number around 200,000 people, living in and around Baliem. "Dani" is a catchall for an array of related linguistic and cultural groups. There are some 30 distinct Dani clans and four distinct language groups spoken in the area.

BELOW Baliem locals at a festival in Wamena. Although the valley has been drawn into the modern world through the activities of Christian missionaries and the Indonesian state over the last half century, a powerful sense of Dani cultural identity remains, and such performances are not simply laid on as tourist spectacles.

ABOVE The Baliem Valley is home to an ancient and fully settled agricultural society quite unlike the hunter-gathering and shifting agriculture traditions found in other parts of Papua. In the countryside many Dani still live close to their gardens in the thatched houses known as *honai*, better insulated against both heat and cold than modern concrete and tin houses.

RIGHT Baliem's cool mountain landscapes, with their thatched farming hamlets and drystone walls, are quite unlike anywhere else in Indonesia, more reminiscent at times of upland areas of Britain and Ireland than of Java and Bali. A complex network of trails connects settlements in the outer parts of the valley away from Wamena, making this superb hiking territory. Traveling here on foot is the best way to experience local Dani life, with village homestays available in many places.

A journey through Indonesia can be as long or as short, as rough or as smooth as you choose to make it. One thing is certain, however. Even on the most extended and ambitious of trips you can only ever expect to see a tiny fraction of what this epic archipelago has to offer.

ACCOMMODATIONS

Accommodation options in Indonesia range from sublime resorts, hidden away amongst rice fields or perched on the edge of powdery white sand, to simple homestays in family compounds. Bali, undoubtedly, offers the best value and most sophisticated service whatever your budget. Elsewhere things tend to be a little more basic and a little less stylish in all price ranges, but better transport links from the center have prompted outlying provinces to up their accommodation games. The diving industry, in particular, has provided the seed for some fabulous resorts to sprout like pearls in the most far-flung corners of the archipelago. For Java, Bali and large cities elsewhere, Internet booking is often possible in all budget ranges. Further afield, telephone booking can be more reliable.

ENTRY POINTS

For long-haul air travelers Indonesia has two main points of entry: Jakarta and Bali. The airports here have links to all corners of Asia, Australia and the Middle East and beyond to Europe and America, as well as the most extensive onwards domestic air connections. However, they are not the only places through which to enter the country. The phenomenally extensive regional flight network within Southeast Asia connects many smaller Indonesian cities with Singapore and Kuala Lumpur. If you're traveling to Indonesia from outside the region and are looking to sidestep Bali and Java, it can sometimes make most sense to use Singapore or KL as your long-haul destination and then book a regional flight onwards from there to Sumatra, Sulawesi or wherever it may be.

The rise of budget air travel means that very few people now reach Indonesia by sea. There are still regular ferries between Singapore and the neighboring Riau islands, but these aren't a very useful entry point for onward travel into Indonesia. Overland entry is still available from Malaysian Borneo, East Timor and Papua New Guinea.

GETTING AROUND

The comfort of travel in Indonesia varies wildly from region to region. In Java there are well-maintained highways plied by air-conditioned coaches as well as an extensive rail network. In the outer reaches of Nusa Tenggara, meanwhile, you're more likely to find yourself trapped in a rock-hard seat in a rattletrap bus as it lurches from pothole to pothole.

The increasingly comprehensive domestic air transport network has made life much easier for those exploring the outlying provinces once reached only on excruciatingly long public ferry rides. Cities throughout Java and Sumatra and regional capitals elsewhere are well served by short-haul jets, with flights often bookable online. Once you get out into the more remote regions, especially in Maluku, Nusa Tenggara and Papua, air transport is more likely to be by small propeller-driven aircraft, with imprecise schedules and complex booking procedures.

HEALTH

Java and Bali generally pose few exotic threats to health beyond the inevitable possibility of minor stomach upsets due to unfamiliar food. In many other parts of Indonesia, however, there is a risk of malaria and other tropical ailments. It's very much worth taking professional medical advice before traveling wherever you plan to visit, as vaccinations may be recommended. For trips to Papua and remote parts of Maluku, Kalimantan and Nusa Tenggara, in particular, doctors may suggest anti-malarial medication.

LANGUAGE

Traditionally English has not been widely spoken in Indonesia, but in major tourist destinations like Bali and in big cities with well-educated populations, many people do now speak excellent English. Even in more remote regions, it's becoming more common to encounter a certain amount of basic English. What's more, Indonesian people are almost always very accommodating and will do their best to figure out what you want, even if they can't understand a word you're saying! That said, it is very much worth learning a bit of Bahasa Indonesia, otherwise known simply as "Indonesian". At a basic level it's one of the most accessible Asian languages for English speakers (no tones or unfamiliar sounds and no new script to decipher) and stocking up on even a simple vocabulary will gain you a very warm response wherever you go.

PLANNING

The first and most important thing to bear in mind when planning a journey through Indonesia is the idea that less is more. Though the domestic flight network has expanded exponentially in the last couple of decades, making non-linear Indonesian journeys far more feasible, just because an itinerary is possible won't necessarily make it preferable. Too much time trotting to and from regional air transport hubs, for example places like Ambon, Medan, Kupang and Jayapura, means too much time overnighting in uninspiring urban centers and too little time in the places you have actually come to see. On a visit of less than a month it is almost always best to stick to no more than two regions, possibly adding a third specific destination if it has direct air access, such as the Komodo National Park as a side trip from Bali. Even Java and Bali, relatively small islands by Indonesian standards, could easily take up a month of your time apiece.

VISAS

Indonesia changes its visa regulations with frustrating frequency. In recent years, however, travelers from many countries have been able to visit for up to a month without needing to obtain a visa in advance, being granted either a free or a pa: ID 30-day visa-on-arrival depending on their specific nationality, or a visa-free 30-day entry stamp if they are citizens of neighboring ASEAN member states. Visas-on-arrival are sometimes extendable for an additional 30 days, but if you're planning a visit of more than a month it's usually better to apply for a 60-day visa in advance from an Indonesian consulate in your home country or in Singapore or Malaysia.

PICTURE CREDITS

Front Cover: ID 115097959 © Pigprox I Shutterstock.com; 42342610 © szefei I Shutterstock.com; ID 526036593 © MarcoMarchi I iStock.com; ID 46643308 © CHEN WS / Shutterstock.com; ID 31735999 © Szefei I Dreamstime.com; **Back Cover**: ID 41051880 © Fabio Lamanna I 123rf.com; ID 94292068 © Dede Dewi I pixoto.com; **Front Endpapers**: ID 118331733 @ Githa Adhi Pramana I Pixoto; **Inside Pages**: p1: ID Sasandu, Traditional palm-leaft harp from Roti, Nusa Tenggara @ Tim Hannigan; p2: ID: 289685645 © Alexander Mazurkevich I Shutterstock.com; p6: ID 73504683 © lesly I Fotolia.com; p8: ID 155280401 © andersen_oystein I iStock.com; p8: ID 172514168 © MsLightBox I iStock.com; p9: ID 182834284 © yai112 I iStock.com; p10: ID 586932576 © Yamtono_Sardi I iStock.com; p11: ID 5740743275577344 © Noer Adie I Pixoto.com; p11: ID 119592587 © Andre Monaf I Pixoto.com; p12: ID 118813687 © Distinctivelmages I iStock.com; p12: ID 794737885 © Sudarsani Ida Ayu Putu I Shutterstock.com; p13: ID 23092725 © Lili Natalia I Pixoto.com; p13: ID 520439747 © Goddard_Photography I iStock.com; p14: ID 458978187 © zodebala I iStock.com; p14: ID © 38103482 Dodohawe I Dreamstime.com; p14: ID 458960455 © zodebala I iStock.com; p14: ID 724163278 © antoni halim I Shutterstock.com; p14: ID 64598953 © Surz01 I Dreamstime.com; p15: ID 698355744 © PRADEEP87 I iStock.com; p15: ID 35783743 © Hafiz Ismail I 123rf.com; p16: ID 340343771 © Reuben Teo I Shutterstock.com; p17: ID 186924582 © mtcurado I iStock.com; p18: ID 336159143 © Zoltan Katona I Shutterstock.com: p18: ID 488874832 © mtcurado I iStock.com; p19: ID British fort, Bengkulu Sumatra © Tim Hannigan; p19: ID 498630775 © NNehring I iStock.com; Page: 19: ID British cannon Bengkulu Sumatra © Tim Hannigan; p20: ID 952640292 © MielPhotos2008 I iStock.com; p20: ID 182836028 © laughingmango I iStock.com; p20: ID 530559275 © dinozaver I iStock.com; p21: ID 458883795 © Herianus I iStock.com; p21: ID 183847811 © laughingmango I iStock.com; p21: ID 504795368 © holgs I iStock.com; Page: 22 Kopi Luwak © Tim Hannigan; p22: ID: 125006796 © Fathur Rahman I Pixoto.com; p23: ID 526808871 © Goddard_Photography I iStock.com; p23: ID 157379044 © georgeclerk I iStock.com; p23: ID 175546255 © laughingmango I iStock.com; p23: ID 471466925 © laughingmango I iStock.com; p24: ID 6355467653087232 © Rahmat Nugroho I Pixoto.com; p26: ID 71148642 © PLAINVIEW I iStock.com; p26: ID 5779098313424896 © Hilmi Photowork I Pixoto.com; p27: ID 70992188 © Adriana Adinandra I Dreamstime.com; p27: ID Tim Hannigan Rotinese ikat, Nusa Tenggara © Tim Hannigan; p28: ID 135008875 © Herru Setiawan I Pixoto; p29: ID 524773461 © Goddard_Photography I iStock.com; p29: ID 44802238 © Yoshi2 I Dreamstime.com; p30: ID 16463878 © Askwhy Wahyoe I Pixoto.com; p30: ID 459021003 © Kerrick I iStock.com; p30: ID 68083602 © rawstudios I Fotolia.com; p31: ID 92495956 © Adee Irawan I Pixoto.com; p31: ID 6508112571793408 © Prince Dastan I Pixoto.com; p32: ID 157436273 © Freder I iStock.com; p33: ID 66338685 © Jeffry Surianto I Pixoto.com; p33: ID 5297738279288832 © Herpin Hendriadi I Pixoto.com; p33: ID 464542817 © decisiveimages I iStock.com; p34: ID 521490109 © Goddard_Photography I iStock.com;Page 35: ID 176901690 © javarman3 I iStock.com; p35: ID 68083602 © rawstudios I Fotolia.com; p35: ID 108200140 © THEPALMER I iStock.com; p36: ID 633111986 © Herdik Herlambang I Shutterstock.com; p39: ID 724322338 © Valery Bocman I Shutterstock.com; p39: ID Mural Detail © Tim Hannigan; p40: ID 31373356 © Daxiao Productions I Shutterstock.com; p40: ID 155745356 © milosk50 I Shutterstock.com; p40: ID 781516675 © Herdik Herlambang I Shutterstock.com; p41: ID 661855717 © Andreas H I Shutterstock.com; p41: ID 85268261 © Dennis Van De Water I Dreamstime.com; p41: ID 84436964 © Yus Ardhiansyah I Pixoto.com; p42: ID 80892617 © Dedesulaiman16 I Dreamstime.com; p42: ID 72603872 © Idris Idris I Dreamstime.com; p42: ID 638611658 © xenovon I iStock.com; p43: ID 43300325 © Danielal I Dreamstime.com; p43: ID 20070858 © Romi Roman I Pixoto.com; p43: ID 15628653 © F.N. Hendrawan I Pixoto.com; p44: ID 751919620 © Marius Dobilas I Shutterstock.com; p44: ID 473672654 © Boogich I iStock.com; p45: ID 182673755 © yai112 I iStock.com; p45: ID 82045326 © Johan Kusuma I 123rf.com; p45: ID 35542817 © Garudeya I Dreamstime.com; p46: ID 426074680 © Perfect Lazybones I Shutterstock.com; p46: ID 503130664 © Kanuman I Shutterstock.com; p46: ID Detail Prambanan_ Central Java © Tim Hannigan; p47: ID 459091177 © Bule Sky Studio I Shutterstock.com; p47: ID Borobudur: Golden Tales of Buddha ISBN: 978-0-8048-4856-5 ® Tuttle Publishing; p48: ID 709492282 © Cak Suud I Shutterstock.com; p48: ID 42177749 © Suryo I Dreamstime.com; p48: ID 1018418338 © Galina Savina I Shutterstock.com; p49: ID 504758704 © noegrr I iStock.com; p49: ID 6188380596994048 © Iman S I Pixoto.com; p50: ID 5833196475252736 © Kamajaya Shagir I Pixoto.com; p50: ID 1060925921 © raditya I Shutterstock.com; p50: ID 592929866 © Farris Noorzali I Shutterstock.com; p51: ID 56339553 © Amsi Rahmanta I Pixoto.com; p51: ID 732657298 © INDONESIAPIX I Shutterstock.com; p52: ID 783045388 © Jarung H I Shutterstock.com; p52: ID 483287995 © wihteorch: ID I iStock.com; p53: ID 49860182 © rumandawi I 123rf.com; p53: ID 5369320037154816 © Punai Cita Cemara I Pixoto.com; p55: ID 533226841 © joakimbkk I iStock.com; p55: ID 34586006 © Irynarasko I Dreamstime.com; p56: ID 689883112 © DmitryVPetrenko I iStock.com; p56: ID 513636770 © RibeirodosSantos I iStock.com; p56: ID 71635441 © Cocosbounty I Dreamstime.com; p56: ID 459001835 © holgs I iStock.com; p57: ID 458676485 © LP7 I iStock.com; p57: ID 109720657 © Arand I iStock.com; p58: ID 524773377 © Goddard_Photography I iStock.com; p58: ID 33682914 © Kevin Fardella I Pixoto.com; p58: ID 562609909 © fotoinfot I Shutterstock.com; p59: ID 86346277 © Constantin Stanciu I Shutterstock.com; p59: ID 68344434 © Dudarev Mikhail I Shutterstock.com; p60; ID 163046672 © Luciano Mortula - LGM I Shutterstock.com; p60: ID 163673850 © kerriekerr I iStock.com; p60: ID 472081465© Nikada I iStock.com; p61: ID 378694603 © Yuki Takahashi I Shutterstock.com; p61: ID 353925716 © Olesya Kuznetsova I Shutterstock.com; p61: ID 30150274 © Blossfeldia I Dreamstime.com; p62: ID 138012338 © tr3gin I Shutterstock.com; p62: ID 232243198 © Attila JANDI I Shutterstock.com; p63: ID 556420267 © Dudarev Mikhail I Shutterstock.com; p63: ID 123331876 © OutdoorWorks I Shutterstock.com; p63: ID 477989317 © Csondy I iStock.com; p64: ID 129005947 © valentinayupov I Fotolia.com; p64: ID 100536202 ® Dudarev Mikhail I Shutterstock.com; p65: ID 93010279 © TerryJLawrence I iStock.com; p65: ID 366608276 © Dan83 I Shutterstock.com; p66: ID 631736717 © Guitar photographer I Shutterstock.com; p66: ID 406630510 © KeongDaGreat I Shutterstock.com; p66: ID 434417845 © GlebSStock I Shutterstock.com; p67: ID 679524784 © IRIT I Shutterstock.com; p67: ID 164823144 © tropicalpixsingapore I iStock.com; p67: ID 172898989 © MsLightBox I iStock.com; p68: ID 506702560 © holgs I iStock.com; p68-69: ID 6259720123318272 © Eko Wijayanto I Pixoto.com; p69: ID 27552320 © Wachirakl I Dreamstime.com; p69: ID 425464777 © GlebSStock I Shutterstock.com; p70: ID 528101345 © joakimbkk I iStock.com; p71: ID 521669631 © Goddard_Photography I iStock.com; p72: ID 6407518608687104 © Didik Mahsyar I Pixoto.com; p72: ID 17069259 © erikj57 I 123rf.com; p72: ID 16835590 © Dudarev Mikhail I Shutterstock.com; p73: ID 5325321899343872 © Ham: ID Mukhlis I Pixoto.com; p73: ID 765007618 © nasrul hisham I Shutterstock.com; p73: ID 96162577 © Wei Hao Ho I Pixoto.com; p74: ID 577537642 © GaudiLab I Shutterstock.com; p74: ID 1035417634 © Eszter Szadeczky-Kardoss I Shutterstock.com; p74: ID 188961530 © Dudarev Mikhail I Shutterstock.com; p74: ID 22776530 © holgs I iStock.com; p74: ID 611070384 © Holger Mette I iStock.com; p75: ID 707790706 © CatwalkPhotos I Shutterstock.com; p75: ID 4834214162726912 © Andi Hermansyah I Pixoto.com; p75: ID 277252721 © Rafal Cichawa I Shutterstock.com; p75: ID 467520964 © benedek I iStock.com; p76: ID 597195260 © Sergey Uryadnikov I Shutterstock.com; p76: ID 5784563130302464 © Abdulgani Atsigah I Pixoto.com; p76: ID 51196776 © aleskolodej I Fotolia.com; p77: ID 4896271827468288 © Leonardus Nyoman I Pixoto.com; p77: ID 53548711 © Svetlin Yosifov I Dreamstime.com; p77: ID 24070563 © Piero Cruciatti I Dreamstime.com; p78: ID Harvesting Lontar Sabu © Tim Hannigan; p78: ID 56742060 © pablitoos I Fotolia.com; p78: ID Larantuka, Flores © Tim Hannigan; p79: ID 152690144 © Carlos Amarillo I Shutterstock.com; p79: ID Takpala village, Alor, Nusa Tenggara © Tim Hannigan; p79: ID Lembata © Tim Hannigan; p80: ID 77517232 © Rafal Cichawa I Shutterstock.com; p80: ID 271945793 © Rafal Cichawa I Shutterstock.com; p80: ID 266331269 © Rafal Cichawa I Shutterstock.com; p80: ID 279072371 © Rafal Cichawa I Shutterstock.com; p81: ID 38238821 © Nikol Senkyrikova I Dreamstime.com; p81: ID 965099744 © faizzaki I iStock.com; p81: ID 61007841 © trubavink I Fotolia.com; p82: ID 34226626 © Rafal Cichawa I Dreamstime.com; p82: ID 1043155474 © KiwiGraphy Studio I Shutterstock.com; p83: ID 489786804 © shannonstent I iStock.com; p83: ID 530459925 © kiats I iStock.com; p84: ID 458604113 © laughingmango I iStock.com; p84: ID 155605298 © milosk50 I Shutterstock.com; p84: ID 183981973 © NattyPTG I iStock.com; p85: ID 357636785 © Sergey Uryadnikov I Shutterstock.com; Page: 85: ID 716291725 © Vladislav T. Jirousek I Shutterstock.com; p85-86: ID 8508558 © Tan Wei Ming I Dreamstime.com; p8: ID 183799471 © laughingmango I iStock.com; p86: ID 73639259 © Tayfun Sertan Yaman I Dreamstime.com; p86: ID 169415438 © Valery Shanin I Shutterstock.com; p86: ID 513786445 © GNNick I iStock.com; p87: ID 183853839 © laughingmango I iStock.com; p87: ID 28922664 © Rezaphotograph I Dreamstime.com; p88: ID 5690854483689472 © Deni Dahnie I Pixoto.com; p88: ID 6290387828211712 © Fathar Alex I Pixoto.com; p88: ID 5438196515078144 © Syafriadi S Yatim I Pixoto.com; p89: ID 91917122 © Gery Arsuma I Pixoto.com; p89: ID 678074407 © ismed_photography_SS I Shutterstock.com; p89: ID 125116469 © Indra M Hutabarat I Pixoto.com; p89: ID 489788082 © shannonstent I iStock.com; p89: ID 157728253 © DavorLovincic I iStock.com; p90: ID 31566267© fusiondub I Depositphotos.com; p90: ID 117093719 © Gwmb2013 I Dreamstime.com; p90: ID 58341076 © Aliaksandr Mazurkevich I Dreamstime.com; p91: ID 92276080 © Sonyasgar I Dreamstime.com; p91: ID 88387492 © Andris Hengki Piciza I Dreamstime.com; p91: ID 95635219 © Rahmad Himawan I Dreamstime.com; p91: ID 21073134 © elikova I Dreamstime.com; p92: ID 5004456115044352 © Yopie Rantau I Pixoto.com; p93: ID 98114226 © gudkovandrey I Fotolia.com; p93: ID 20467803 © Rafal Cichawa I Dreamstime.com; p94: ID 172879661 © MsLightBox I iStock.com; p94: ID 285272471 © Rafal Cichawa I Shutterstock.com; p94: ID 34_Kantong_ Semar_Highland_Rain_Forest_Papua-Indonesia.jpg © WidodoMargotomo I Commons.wikimedia.org; p95: ID 34309419 © Rafal Cichawa I Fotolia.com; p95: ID 287639312 © Rafal Cichawa I Shutterstock.com; p95: ID 57619960 © Hong Ki Kim I Dreamstime.com; p95: ID 35542050 © Garudeya I Dreamstime.com; p96: ID 471898795 © guenterguni I iStock.com; p96: ID 441022744 © JMcurto I Shutterstock.com; p97: ID 5237293937852416 © Rifki Muslim I Pixoto.com; p97: ID 60696665 © Mukhtarfuaddi I Dreamstime.com; p97: ID 525497435 © benedek I iStock.com; p98: ID 96495203 © Johan Kusuma I Dreamstime.com; p98: ID 781839874 © cendhika I Shutterstock.com; p99: ID 19859075 © Ari Sanjaya I Dreamstime.com; p99: ID 47029431 © Fenkie Sumolang I Dreamstime.com; p99: ID 280396334 © Rafal Cichawa I Shutterstock.com; p99: ID 39066806 © Nizar Kauzar I Pixoto.com; p100: ID 18854912 © Deny Ariyanto I Pixoto.com; p101: ID 173421992 © ifish I iStock.com; p102: ID 371674639 © Elena Odareeva I Shutterstock.com; p102: ID 53674443 © suronin I Fotolia.com; p103: ID 176010342 © Jot I iStock.com; p103: ID 5629928229830656 © Simon Quek I Pixoto.com; p104: ID 361856729 © javarman I Shutterstock.com; p104: ID 499699542 © benedek I iStock.com; p105: ID 53747934 © Rafal Cichawa I Dreamstime.com; p105: ID 21591255 © Jakub Cejpek I Dreamstime.com; p105: ID 515167996 © Salparadis I Shutterstock.com; p106: ID 53791131 © pablitoos I Fotolia.com; p106: ID 69248595 © Elena Odareeva I Dreamstime.com; p107: ID 207079393 © Kristina Vackova I Shutterstock.com; p107: ID 155154407 © ifish I iStock.com; p107: ID 40724006 © Asiantraveler I Dreamstime.com; p107: ID 400989193 © Elena Odareeva I Shutterstock.com; p108: ID 775687384 © raditya I Shutterstock.com; p108: ID 296872940 © fenkieandreas I Shutterstock.com; p108: ID 226474399 © enkieandreas I Shutterstock.com; p109: ID 70538987 © Artushfoto I Dreamstime.com; p109: ID 277680452 © Dudarev Mikhail I Shutterstock.com; p109: ID 18477780 © Daexto I Dreamstime.com; p109: ID 43696174 © Fenkie Sumolang I Dreamstime.com; p109: ID 1018027576 © DJ Mattaar I Shutterstock.com; p110: ID 42451837 © Joris Croese I 123rf.com; p110: ID 5059488353615872 © Abdul Aziz I Pixoto.com; p111: ID 42452176 © Joris Croese I 123rf.com; p111: ID 622801976 © Edmund Lowe Photography I Shutterstock.com; p112: ID 245186575 © fenkieandreas I Shutterstock.com; p112: ID 530518435 © kiats I iStock.com; p112: ID 84499638 © Edmund Lowe I Dreamstime.com; p112: ID 93365081 © Insos Kampung I Dreamstime.com; p113: ID 1076912927 © Stephane Bidouze I Shutterstock.com; p113: ID 757113289 © Michal Hlavica I Shutterstock.com; p113: ID 6115395858595840 © Nato Revolusi Leisubun I Pixoto.com; p114: ID 535377597 © NNehring I iStock.com; p114: ID 42452052 © Joris Croese I 123RF .com; p115: ID 146868074 © javarman3 I iStock.com; p115: ID 43482841 © Joris Croese I 123rf.com; p115: ID 73760663 © fenkieandreas I Fotolia.com; p115: ID 497465937 © NNehring I iStock.com; p116: ID 4695090014453760 © Sofarianty Agustin I Pixoto.com; p116: ID 41768306 © Mahdy Muchammad I Pixoto.com; p117: ID 6450300857090048 © Fahriadi Yusuf Abdulfattah I Pixoto.com; p117: ID 52036223 © Tomy Nurseta Widyadi I Dreamstime.com; p117: ID 68724369 © Abdinillah Massa I Pixoto.com; p117: ID 120073583 © Vincensius Yudhistira Lindung Setiyana I Pixoto.com; p118: ID 112079639 © Sergey Uryadnikov / Shutterstock.com; p119: ID 26381879 © Sergey Uryadnikov I Dreamstime.com; p119: ID 36946053 © Sergey Uryadnikov I Dreamstime.com; p120: ID 63067891 © Michael Mücke I Fotolia.com; p120: ID 107686697 © andamanse I Fotolia.com; p121: ID 5637575974322176 © Dikye Darling I Pixoto.com; p121: ID 48053848 © Sergey Uryadnikov I Dreamstime.com; p121: ID 70104740 © Sergey Uryadnikov I Dreamstime.com; p121: ID 64092557 © Sergey Uryadnikov I Dreamstime.com; p122: ID 50078590 © Petr Zamecnik I Dreamstime.com; p122: ID 4784705480163328 © Sofi Sugiharto I Pixoto.com; p122: ID 126504156 © Donny Irawan I Pixoto.com; p123: ID 4670197248032768 © Donny Irawan I Pixoto.com; p123: ID 6035698246221824 © Geoffrey Saturnus I Pixoto.com; p123: ID 59802984 © axfi1 I Fotolia.com; p124: ID 37611357 © Sengkiu Pasaribu I Pixoto.com; p124: ID 30365970 © Danemo I Dreamstime.com; p125: ID 5738453792718848 © Semuel Angga Angga I Pixoto.com; p125: ID 66049994 © Andrey Gudkov I 123rf.com; p125: ID 6581955841753088 © Muchamad Irfan I Pixoto.com; p125: ID 96190381 © andersen_oystein I iStock.com; p125: ID 105407808 © Pavel Glazkov I Pixoto.com; **Back Endpapers**: ID 852092422 © Todikromo I iStock.com

Published by Tuttle Publishing, an imprint
of Periplus Editions (HK) Ltd

www.tuttlepublishing.com

Copyright © 2018 Periplus Editions (HK) Limited

ISBN: 978-0-8048-4711-7

Distributed by
North America, Latin America & Europe
Tuttle Publishing
364 Innovation Drive
North Clarendon, VT 05759-9436 U.S.A.
Tel: 1 (802) 773-8930; Fax: 1 (802) 773-6993
info@tuttlepublishing.com; www.tuttlepublishing.com

Japan
Tuttle Publishing
Yaekari Building, 3rd Floor
5-4-12 Osaki
Shinagawa-ku
Tokyo 141-0032
Tel: (81) 3 5437-0171; Fax: (81) 3 5437-0755
sales@tuttle.co.jp; www.tuttle.co.jp

Asia Pacific
Berkeley Books Pte. Ltd.
3 Kallang Sector, #04-01/02
Singapore 349278
Tel: (65) 6280-1330; Fax: (65) 6280-6290
inquiries@periplus.com.sg; www.periplus.com

Indonesia
PT Java Books Indonesia
Kawasan Industri Pulogadung
JI. Rawa Gelam IV No. 9
Jakarta 13930
Tel: (62) 21 4682-1088; Fax: (62) 21 461-0206
crm@periplus.co.id; www.periplus.com

22 21 20 19 18   10 9 8 7 6 5 4 3 2 1

Printed in China
1810CM

ABOUT TUTTLE: BOOKS TO SPAN THE EAST AND WEST

Our core mission at Tuttle Publishing is to create books which
bring people together one pat a time. Tuttle was founded in 1832
in the small New England town of Rutland, Vermont (USA). Our
fundamental values remain as strong today as they were then—to
publish best-in-class books informing the English-speaking world
about the countries and peoples of Asia. The world has become
a smaller place today and Asia's economic, cultural and political
influence has expanded, yet the need for meaningful dialogue and
information about this diverse region has never been greater. Since
1948, Tuttle has been a leader in publishing books on the cultures,
arts, cuisines, languages and literatures of Asia. Our authors
and photographers have won numerous awards and Tuttle has
published thousands of books on subjects ranging from martial
arts to paper crafts. We welcome you to explore the wealth of
information available on Asia at **www.tuttlepublishing.com**.

BACK ENDPAPERS Bound for home: as the sun slips down in the
direction of Sumbawa, Lombok, Bali and Java, a boat threads its
way through the islands of the Komodo National Park, heading for
port. Though this particular boat has been built to carry sightseers
and divers, its design follows the ancient *pinisi* pattern pioneered
by the Bugis shipwrights of Sulawesi. Bugis boats have been passing
through the waters around Komodo for hundreds of years, en route
for the ports of Sumba and Timor to purchase valuable sandalwood,
or still further, beyond the far horizon, to the northern reaches of
Australia to gather sea cucumbers to sell to Chinese traders and to
barter with the local Aboriginals.